T0147254

GOD

ARE YOU TALKING TO ME?

One Identity's Journey to Spiritual Awakening

DR. TANA TILLMAN

BALBOA.
PRESS

Balboa Press books may be ordered through booksellers or by contacting:

Balboa Press
A Division of Hay House
1663 Liberty Drive
Bloomington, IN 47403
www.balboapress.com
1-(877) 407-4847

Because of the dynamic nature of the Internet, any Web addresses or links contained in this book may have changed since publication and may no longer be valid. The views expressed in this work are solely those of the author and do not necessarily reflect the views of the publisher, and the publisher hereby disclaims any responsibility for them.

The author of this book does not dispense medical advice or prescribe the use of any technique as a form of treatment for physical, emotional, or medical problems without the advice of a physician, either directly or indirectly. The intent of the author is only to offer information of a general nature to help you in your quest for emotional and spiritual well-being. In the event you use any of the information in this book for yourself, which is your constitutional right, the author and the publisher assume no responsibility for your actions.

ISBN: 978-1-4525-0093-5 (sc)
ISBN: 978-1-4525-0162-8 (e)
Printed in the United States of America
Balboa Press rev. date: 11/17/10

For all the people on this
journey with me.

"And so it begins. With our hearts and minds in tune we all begin a journey."

Jeanie Gibson

Author's Preface

Hello, my name is Tana (pronounced like the last two syllables of Montana) Tillman. I wrote the book you are about to read over a period of twelve weeks of my life while studying and practicing the prescribed Lessons in *A Course in Miracles*. If this book has come to you, then I believe God wants you to read it. I hope that you hear God talking to you from it and receive all of His/Her Blessings. Neither God nor I (I believe) want this to be the only book you read about a person's experience of coming nearer to Your Father/Mother. You should read many different people's experiences. In these diverse readings you will discover that some are neither accepted nor found in traditional churches' dogmas today, yet you will begin to see common threads that run through all of the authors who are hearing God's voice today. Here are some major threads that I have found that run through people's experiences in this quest to come closer to God that ring true to me, and if they do not make your heart sing it might not be the time for you to read this particular book. For I truly feel that I am hearing these Truths:

- God is talking to everyone today, not just 2,000 years ago.

- There is one Divine Source, and it does not matter what your name for It is or if you believe in God.

- God is Love.

- God wants us to love everybody including ourselves.

- God does not mete out punishment.

- God is the Union of all living things.

- Each of us is on a journey to return home to be one with our Father/Mother and each and every one of us will be successful.

- Each of us has the ability to access the Christ Mind and use it to bless others and oneself.

- God wants Her/His children to only experience peace and joy at all times and beyond time.

This book is written as a log of the twelve weeks in my life beginning with the time in which I heard that small, quiet voice tell me to write this book. I have started each day or week with a conversation with God. I have used the words *Self* to precede what I thought or said. I have left the Words of God out in the conversations. I have done that purposefully, because I want you to hear what God is saying. You can hear Her. All you have to do is set aside a regular time each morning and evening in which you are still and quiet. All I have done is something that each and every one of you can do, too.

After each conversation is a description of the events that occurred during my life at that time that confirm my belief that I heard God, followed His instructions, and received Her blessings. I have never been as peaceful and joyful in my life, as I am at this time. I now look at each occurrence in my life as an opportunity to give or receive God's blessing, whereas in the past I would have ranted and railed at God and questioned Her reason for this happening to me. Today I realize that if something is too hard for me to do and is not bringing me peace and joy, then it probably is not what God wants me to do. Now this does not mean that I will not work hard to accomplish what I think He wants me to do, but it just means that I take the path He has opened up for me that brings me more peace and joy. On this journey, I still have a long way to go. I still have challenges and am still working diligently on preventing mean thoughts from entering into my mind. The ego tries very desperately to keep me chained to this earth and constantly tempts me to prevent me from reaching my Mother/Father, but I know I can do it with more practice and with the Grace of God.

This book is one person's documentation of the blessings you can receive and give, if you listen to God. I hope this book blesses you in reading it, as it has me by writing it. Happy reading and may God Bless you each and every One!

Table of Contents

1
Day One

God, are you talking to me? You want me to write a book?

Self: God, did I really hear you say you wanted me to write a book?

Self: God, I know you are all powerful and everything, but you can't mean me!

Self: Yes, I was that good student who took advanced English classes and always got her papers turned back without any red "X"s in front of mistakes for grammar or mechanics. But, remember there was always that comment in red across the top of the paper. Don't you remember those words Mrs. Watkins had written (I know I will never forget), "Sounds like something a first grader would write." You can't expect me to write a book, my teacher told me I couldn't write!

1

Self: But God, I am not worthy of being your scribe. I'm just a normal person. Who would want to read something I wrote? I didn't study theology.

Self: Yes God, I went to church every Sunday in my younger years. You know the one, the Presbyterian Church. It was in that quiet loving church that I learned to be still and to begin to listen and hear Your Voice.

Self: And yes, I did get the Baptist perspective when I visited Granny. There I heard Reverend Burrell's interpretation of what he thought were Your Words in a booming voice. That's also where I was frightened to death by his voice telling me the Devil was always trying to tempt me and if I wasn't good I was going to hell.

Self: You're right God; I studied the Bible and learned many verses which I can still recite today. But, there were things in there that didn't make sense to me. You know, like how did Cain and Able find wives if they were the sons of Adam and Eve, the first people? Where did those wives come from?

Self: But, I certainly know You know I haven't attended a church regularly since my college days. I did go just a few weeks ago when I was at Aunt Jean's house. I went with her to that little Methodist Church near her, and I really thoroughly enjoyed it! I really like a female minister's perspective much more than a male's! Why don't You have more women in Your pulpits? To me their message is more like the one I think You want to get out there. You know the message about LOVE.

Self: You're right, again as always! While I was watching Aunt Jean's pastor, I received Your first sign that You sent for me to know that I was doing what You wanted me to do. I saw that beautiful glow You shone around her body. It appeared to be glowing about 6 or 7 inches beyond her physical body. I certainly was glad You sent me that sign! I needed the physical reassurance that I had found favor in Your Eyes.

Self: God, but are You sure it's me You want to do this? I am not an important person, and I am a girl. I know You don't even see gender, but out here in the 21st century there are still churches that make a big deal about gender and don't even allow females to perform certain duties and responsibilities!

Self: God, I can't do this. I am not worthy of writing Your words. I am from just a middle class family. You know I was raised in the suburbs in the 1950's and 60's. My dad was one of those heroic people that had served in WW II and worked 3 jobs to give us what we had. My mom worked many jobs, too and only one of them was for money outside of our home. She was a secretary. Remember then, that a woman could only be a secretary, nurse, teacher, or homemaker. I know You heard my thoughts about what I wanted to be when I grew up. I didn't want to do any of those jobs that society had pigeon-holed women into doing. I wanted to be an archaeologist! Now if I had become a famous archaeologist who had made some startling discoveries, then someone would have paid to read one of my books. You know also that that never happened, because I changed my mind about wanting to be an archaeologist as soon as I realized that most of an archaeologist's work is done in VERY HOT places, I knew then that job was not the one for me! That's when I decided to be a teacher like my aunt. I made my poor sister play school all of the time. But, I don't think that being a teacher makes me qualified to write a book. I mean I taught math and science, not even English and history, much less theology!

Self: God, yes You're right once more. I am a voracious reader. My dad did start sitting with me when I first began to read. He did move an index card over each line of words I was trying to read, so my eyes were trained to move on to the next line more rapidly than the average person. If only, he had made it readily available to everyone and made the money the people who started up those first speed reading courses made!

Self: And yes, I have persevered through writing a dissertation to earn my educational doctorate degree. But, this is completely different!

Self: Hey God, are You positive I am the one You want to do this? Okay. Now, I know how Noah felt when you asked him to build The Ark!

Events of Day One

"I can't believe I really am going to do this! Come on, Tana it's no big deal. You do this every day," I say to myself as I get my computer out trying to convince myself that this is just any other normal day in an average person's life. And, I do get out my computer every morning to teach online education courses to aspiring teachers. But, today is different. I am taking a huge leap of faith in believing that this small, still voice in my head is actually God talking to me and directing my path. This leap of faith requires that I actually open up a blank page in Word on my computer and start typing the title of this book on it. Here I go. I take a deep breath and type, "God, Are You Talking to Me: One Identity's Journey to Spiritual Awakening" at the top. There, it is done. Oh wait, no, it is just the beginning like the very beautiful and apt Foreword my friend Jeanie (you'll be more properly introduced to her tomorrow) wrote for this book and didn't know she was writing.

So, what's next? You have your title. That part was easy. It came to me days ago, as a very small thought. It may have been small, yet it was clear in my head. When I woke up and had to start typing this morning, the thought about the name of this book came back to me. I remembered I had thought it. The difference is today the thought just doesn't flit through my mind as a thought. Today, it comes out loud and clear along with the message, "This is the title of the book you are going to write." I didn't really hear a voice, but the message couldn't have been any clearer.

I really have no idea what is next, so I just start writing down ideas about things I don't want to forget to include. Some of it even comes out as entire paragraphs! This is a familiar process to me, because it is the way that I wrote my dissertation. I needed something familiar, as all of the rest of it was pretty strange. By strange, I mean all of the things I was going to talk about here in this book. Of course, strange things have happened to me in my life. Looking back, I see that they were God's plan and a way of easing me into experiencing what other people would call paranormal experiences, but what I call Miracles or God's Love being manifested here on earth.

The first one is centered on my maternal grandmother. To set the background for you for this part of my story, you need to know that my mother almost hemorrhaged to death when my sister, Lynn, who is 22 months younger than me, was born. While mother recuperated at home for months unable to care for herself much less 2 children under the age of 2, I was sent to her mother's house in South Georgia; and my newborn sister went to my mother's cousin, Margaret. Maggie had been a nurse in WW II and was childless. She was elated to carry Lynn on her hip and spoil her rotten, while I was being given extra attention by Granny and my mother's sister, Jean. Jean was 12 when I lived with them for those 3 months. She dressed me up and rode me around in her doll carriage showing me off to anyone who would stop and look at me. Jean is also the aunt to which I refer in my conversations between God and me above, who was the teacher I wanted to emulate when I decided I did not want to be an archaeologist because most of that work is done in very hot temperatures.

I am telling you all of this to set the stage for you to understand the special bond I had with my maternal grandmother. In her later years, my parents had moved to South Georgia in order for my mother to be closer to her mother. All the family holidays were spent at my mom and dad's house on beautiful, Lake Seminole. During one of these events, I remember talking to my grandmother. I was telling her I was so glad she was doing better. She had been diagnosed with diabetes in her later life and had to go on a diet. This woman was known far and wide as a wonderful cook, and she enjoyed what she made (especially those desserts). She had followed the doctor's orders and had lost much weight. She told me that contrary to what I thought, that she wasn't doing well. I reminded her of the doctor's last good report, but her words continued to deny the truth of what her diagnostic tests had concluded.

Later on that same day as we got ready to make the trip back to the suburbs of Atlanta, my second husband (yes, I've been married 3 times – what can I say – just haven't found the right one yet) whose maternal ancestors were American Indian, said to me, "Tana, the next time we come down here will be for a funeral." Now, that really creeped me out! I believed he knew what he was saying, because he had related to me other times in his life when he knew things were going to happen before they happened. I pushed the fright and concern for whose funeral it would be way down deep inside of me and went on with my life.

Sometime later, I was working. At that time I taught elementary school. I don't remember a whole lot about occurrences in my past, because if they were bad I would just have my mind erase the experiences. I had already completely erased all memories of my paternal grandfather (like I didn't even remember calling him Gran-Gran), because I couldn't deal with his death at the age of 5. Anyway, back to that day I am trying to tell you about. I had awakened on that day feeling happy and ready for the day. Normally, you can ask people who know me; I am a pretty upbeat, positive person. Once, I got to school I went about performing my duties and responsibilities as a teacher. Somewhere in the morning, all of that changed. All of the sudden, I felt as if a dark cloud had descended upon me. I have never had this feeling before or afterwards. It was just as if my happy, normal day had turned into a sad, abnormal one. I remember sitting on the stage in the cafeteria where all the teachers sat to watch the children and remarking to those who sat by me about the weird feeling that had come over me.

I had children to teach, so I just kept trudging through the day. I had completely forgotten about it the next day. That next day seemed pretty normal, until I was summoned to the principal's office. Even though I knew I wasn't in trouble, I knew it was a portent of bad things to be called into it. There was a telephone call waiting for me there. Today, I don't know who made it. It was probably my husband or father. Anyway, I had to go to South Georgia to attend my maternal grandmother's funeral. So, the next time I went to my parent's house was for a funeral like my husband had predicted. Now, don't think that is the big paranormal experience, because it isn't. Many people know someone who has experienced precognitive events.

When I got to my parent's, I was told the story about how we heard about her death. It was Friday, and mom went to pick up her mom each week on that day. My mother would drive Granny around town to do her errands, shop, and pay her bills. While my mother was driving that 25 minutes into town to get her, a family friend's maid (no, not the kind that lives in your house because you have money – but the kind that came in once a week to help with the cleaning because you are an older person that needs help) answered a phone call. The person on the other end said she had had a blackout spell or something. She said that when Jane (the family friend) got back from shopping to come over to her house and see about her. She stressed to the maid to not let Jane come alone, but for her to come, too. Soon after that phone call, Jane came home. They got in the car and went to my grandmother's house. When they got there, the screen door in the back was latched. They couldn't get my grandmother to come to the door, so they pulled the screen door open breaking the lock. When they found my grandmother, she was sitting in her favorite chair with her dishes from her lunch on the TV tray beside it. They called for help.

Meanwhile, my mother is driving into town. When she pulls into her mother's driveway, they are putting the body into the ambulance. My mother did not have to find her mother. We were all so grateful, that she did not have to experience finding her that way. Now, that is just another person's story about finding a relative who has passed until you know the rest. Here comes the paranormal part. The next day, the coroner called. It seems my grandmother had been dead for many hours. In fact, she had been dead for so long, that we couldn't have an open coffin funeral. That was another blessing. We all only had to remember her the way we last saw her alive and not lifeless in a coffin.

Later as we were all trying to come to grips with what had happened, I remembered the dark feeling I had had the previous day. I realized that must have been the time that she left this earthly plane. Somewhere, I had known a great sadness when that occurred. I had solved the mystery of the black cloud feelings, but who had made that phone call? We knew it couldn't have been my grandmother. She had been dead. Or, was it her? The family is sure it was my grandmother. We believe her spirit realized that her daughter was on the way to see her. We think my grandmother's love was strong enough to make that phone call in order to prevent my mother from finding her body. Now, what form that phone call took, who knows? **God are you talking to us? Have You sent signs to us to reassure us that Your promise of everlasting life is true?**

The next paranormal experiences or miracle I want to tell you about involve my mother and her leaving this earthly plane. What can I say except, like mother-like daughter.

My mother not only did all those things good mothers do, but she was special. Not only did any of us children ever have a birthday without one of her homemade birthday cakes, but she would bake them for people at work. She would get us to church every Sunday, and then come home and create the most wonderful Sunday meals and this was without stores that were open on Sunday or after 6 o'clock, microwaves, or dishwashers! Mom would volunteer to do things like be in charge of a group of Camp Fire Girls in which my sister or I was in. She made sure we got to dance, choir, and whatever else Lynn and I wanted to do. In other words, I couldn't have had a better one! Then to top it off, as adults she was my best friend! We loved talking about books we had read, liked watching the same TV programs, loved to go to movies, and traveling. Unfortunately, she passed away in this same month in which I am writing this book 3 years ago.

She had been very sick and in much pain for several months before she left us here in her earthly home. This part of the story starts with another one of those phone calls you do not want to receive. We (Waylon - my son, his fiancé, and her daughter, and I) had just left mom and dad's house the day before. I had spent all the time I could at my parent's home at Lake Seminole helping mom during the past six months when she had been so ill, but when the summer was over my job only allowed me to spend the weekends and weeklong breaks down there. During the work week (because my sister works from home), Lynn came to care for mom. We would often pass each other on the road and wave.

Back to the phone call that came about lunch time. When I answered my cell phone at school (again something I usually do not do is have my cell phone on at work), it was Lynn. She said that the wonderful ladies from Hospice had just left and that they did not think mom was going to make it through the night. She had been unconscious since that morning. I told my sister that as soon as I could get there, that I would be there with the knowledge that it would probably be very late after getting everything ready and making the four and a half hour drive.

As soon as I got off the phone, I thought, "But she was the best she had been yesterday when I saw her!" I remembered that just a few hours ago, the two of us had sat on the screened in back porch (remember it's January and my mother had not left the inside of the house except for doctor's appointments for weeks because of her ill health and the back pain) and watched Waylon play with his new found family-to-be. When we had to go back home, mom got up for the first time in a long time and walked us to the door to give us our good bye hugs. Looking back on it, I realize that somewhere inside of her she had found the strength to give us that one last good day before she departed this earth as we know it. Thank you, mom!

After the thought about what a good day the previous one had been, I started trying to think about what I had to get done to get down to be with mom. The first problem was that I was at school without my car! This week we had driven my friend Jeanie's (you know the one you will meet tomorrow, but I guess are meeting today) car to work. As I am crying and trying to think about how I am going to get almost 30 miles back home to get packed to leave without a car, I go to find Jeanie.

As I stand outside her classroom crying, Jeanie hurries out to see to me. I tell her what is going on. I know she will gladly drive me home, but hate to ask her. I hate to ask her, because Jeanie has taken some alternative students under her wings which do not do well without their surrogate mother (Jeanie) watching over them. But I think I have no choice if I am going to get home, until I call my son Waylon. Waylon in his work could be anywhere, yet today when I call him he is no more than a couple of miles down the street in a restaurant eating lunch. Was that just a coincidence with as large as Atlanta and its suburbs are? I don't think so!

Jeanie drives me to meet Waylon. I am elated to find Dana, his fiancé, with him. It is a much better plan (thank you God for Your plan – especially in times like these) that Waylon is driving me home and that on the way we stop and get everything we need to go for an extended stay and prepare for mom's funeral.

Getting everything done before we could leave was not easy. Waylon had to make arrangements for his partner to handle the work they were doing. We had to go to Dana's house to pick up her clothes, and then get her daughter, Jadelyn, from day care and take her to a relative's house to stay while we were gone. After that we had to go to Waylon's house for him to get his stuff and lastly go to mine.

Many hours after the phone call, we finally get on I-75 heading south. Waylon drove my convertible. I sat in the back. I did not want to look at the speedometer, because I did not want to know how fast Waylon was going to go to get to see his Gree one last time. I decided to lie down in the back seat, so I could not see the speedometer and worry about the speed. As I looked out at dusk, the trees seemed to be a dark grey blur. I finally said, "Waylon, you can slow down your Gree will wait for you." At that time, I do not know where that assurance came from, but it was VERY definitely there!

Waylon replied, "But mom, I didn't tell Gree how special she was to me and how much I love her!" Again, I reassured him that she would wait for him.

After what seemed like an eternity, we finally arrived! It was 10:30 or so. Lynn and dad related the events of the day. Since she was unconscious, they had moved mom in her favorite recliner to a position in the great room in front of the TV. We all spoke to her, but there were no replies. As we sat watching TV, I wondered how do you do a death watch? Lynn's body got tired, so she told us she was going to bed. Dad, Waylon, Dana, and I continued to watch mom's unconscious form lay in the reclined chair.

The TV was on Game Show Network. That is what mother had wanted to watch in those last months. I don't know whether it was all the pain medicine she was taking or whether her lovely spirit was spending more time away from this earthly plane than with us, but a 30 minute game show seemed to be all her mind could attend to.

While we were watching TV, reruns of Regis Philbin hosting *Who Wants to be a Millionaire* came on, and it was one of mom's favorite game shows. The first thing we noticed is mother's eyes seemed to be blinking. Earlier when you had pulled her eyelids back, they had been more yellow than green and were cloudy. We kept watching and eventually they were open. I went over and asked her if she wanted anything. She replied, "Uh-uh." I asked her if she was in pain, and again she was able to get out those same 2 syllables. We all knew it was a struggle for her to talk after being unconscious for hours. She sat and watched Regis for a while. At some point she said, "Tee-tee." Dad and Waylon each got on one of her sides and took her to the bathroom. I asked her if she wanted to go to bed, and she nodded her head one time for yes. Dad and Waylon placed her in the bed. Waylon leaned over and said, "I've never told you what a GREAT grandmother you have been to me and how much I love you. I love you Gree." He leaned over and kissed her cheek good-bye. She had waited on him and had come back from her near death to hear those words he needed for her to hear him say. In fact she blessed us all with those moments of consciousness by being able to pretend she was just going to sleep for a night yet giving us each an opportunity to tell her we loved her and kiss her good-bye. And, one last time dad crawled into bed and was able to lie next to the love of his life of almost 57 years.

Once she was not in the beautiful home in Lake Seminole that my dad built for her, it was so difficult for me to travel down there to see dad. I knew he missed her the most, because he was used to her being there. While I was away in the Atlanta suburbs, I could pretend that she was still there waiting for me to visit them, but once I got in the car all I could think about was that she was not there.

My love and concern for my father made me finally talk myself into making the trip. When I got there, dad told me he had vacuumed the floor the previous day to get the house ready for me and to reassure me that he was okay. He said that the only thing that was strange was he found a purple Skittle on the carpet near the front door. He doesn't eat them and knew no one that had been in the house that did. I knew my brother ate them and said so. We decided it must have been him that dropped one. We had a nice visit, and a few hours later we went to bed.

The next morning, I was sitting at the bar (no not the kind in which you imbibe alcoholic drinks- though we have- but the eating bar in the middle of the very large great room) drinking my morning glass of Crystal Light and dad comes in after having breakfast as he does every day with his cronies in the Breakfast Club. He goes to the bar and picks up something. He walks over and hands it to me and says, "This is what I found in the carpet as I was going out the front door this morning." It was a purple skittle. I didn't get it the first time, but I got it the second time! I said, "Dad, I love the Skittles that come in the purple bag. When I would tell mom I was coming, she would buy them and put them in the candy machine (you know the old-fashioned kind where you put the coin in, turn the handle, and candy comes out the spout) for me to have." I know that it was a special gift of love from my mom that said, "Welcome home". Of course, I couldn't make myself eat it and didn't want to leave it as it may draw bugs, so I threw the Skittle away.

When I started telling my story to my sister Lynn, she said that she often asks mother to send her a sign. Lynn says that she has never said that without a butterfly or hummingbird (2 of mother's favorite things in nature – she had a butterfly house and many hummingbird houses) coming into her view.

My brother did not relate his "Mom" story to me until this week. He said that just this past Christmas day he said he told God, "All I want for Christmas this year is a sign from my mother." Right after he said that, an ornament from our parent's house that had been sitting in a box in a corner of his great room began to play its tune.

Now I look for signs that my mom is still with me even though I can't see her, and I find them. Just a few weeks ago, I was helping my dad clean out his house at Lake Seminole after it was sold in preparation for the new owners. I found a plastic bag that had "laundry" written on it with black marker. I opened it up and saw socks. Not just any socks, but brightly colored ones with stripes and a place for each toe! These were the ones my mother loved to wear with her Birkenstocks. Finding that bag filled with many of just those type of socks brought tears of joy to my eyes. To me they were a sign that mother appreciated my being there and helping dad. Thank you, mom.

I hope at this point that I have provided you with enough evidence of strange experiences that you can begin to see that God has been planning for a long time to help me become accustomed to His Miracles of Love that he has for me to experience, if I am just watching for them and believing it is possible.

2
Days Two and Three

God, are you talking to me? You want me to <u>tell</u> people that I'm writing a book?

Self: God, You want me to do WHAT?

Self: Did I hear You say You want me to tell my family and friends that I am going through this weird stuff and putting my experiences down and writing a book about it? They'll think I'm crazy!

Self: God, are You sure? You know I will have to come out of the "New Age" closet! I might as well go out into the streets and shout, "Yes, label me as a New Age believer! I do believe Jesus is with us today, talking to us, and performing miracles!"

Self: Okay, I just guess all of my family and friends will have to be seen looking at books in the "New Age" section.

Self: But God, why can't our book go into the religious section? I feel closer to You and Your son, Jesus, now than I ever have.

Self: God You are right, as You always are. You haven't steered me wrong yet. So, You know I will do what You want me to do.

Events of Days 2 & 3

As all of these thoughts bounced around in my head, I thought about the ramifications of what I was thinking about doing. Deep down inside, I was very scared of being judged, even though one of the major premises in *A Course in Miracles* is to train you not to judge! In fact for a split second, I was MORTIFIED! The thoughts that this very average, southern girl who had spent every Sunday for the first 12 years of her life in a Presbyterian church (yes, I had the pin with a bar for each year of attendance to prove it was so) was feeling really ookey about telling people about her very personal experiences with Jesus, the Son of God.

The first person God set up for me to talk to, was my son, Waylon. To start out how this part of the story unfolded (you know the part where I have to tell my family and friends that God is talking to me) I have to share the other conversation I had with myself after I got off the phone with Waylon. It goes something like this:

Self: Wait a minute. Have I just told my son about all of these weird experiences I have been having?

Self: I don't know what happened! One minute I was having an everyday conversation with my son, and the next thing I know the words were just tumbling out of my mouth.

Self: Why did I do that? He is going to think his momma has lost her mind!

Now, here are the events as they happened that led up to that conversation with myself. It was the 2nd day after beginning this journey of hearing God tell me to record my experiences and of doing so. I again had gotten up and started the day with saying to myself what *A Course in Miracles* says is a good way to start off each day, so I said to myself, "Today I want peace, joy, abundant blessings, and good health. If I make no decisions by myself, then this is the day I will be given." I went to the tab on the internet that I kept open for my lesson. I read it, and closed my eyes to meditate for 5 minutes on that idea that was presented to me from *A Course in Miracles* and listen to hear God's Voice. I went to the next tab that I keep open and was anxious and ready to hear what the Master Teacher (a website I had found on the ACIM website) was going to say to me next. I clicked on the play arrow and began to watch what appeared on the screen.

It began like it always does with what looks like a picture of the universe with a golden sphere across the top and light in the shape of a cross below it streaming out in both directions. Then, what Master Teacher calls "God's Commercial" starts scrolling down the page with my hearing the Master Teacher's voice reading the words. I was ready to go to that peaceful place where I learn more about what God wants me to learn. But, alas that was not meant to be!

You see right after I began to hear the first words from the Master Teacher come out of my computer's speakers, I heard the Calypso ring tone blaring from my phone. That is the ring tone I have set on my phone to tell me my son Waylon is calling. I think that ringtone is just perfect to tell me my high energy son wants to talk to his mother.

For a nanosecond the thought went through my head, "Oh no, not again! Son, you interrupted this same lesson at the same point yesterday! Will I ever get this lesson done?" I said a nanosecond, because right after that thought flitted through my mind *A Course in Miracles* mind training kicked in. I took a deep breath and said to myself, "If you haven't watched this video 2 mornings in a row, then the Holy Spirit is saying you are not ready for this one at this time." So, I hit the pause button and still keeping the peace God promises me with me, I walk over, pick up my phone, press the little green telephone symbol, and say, "Hello" to my son.

Somewhere in our conversation he starts relaying his fears that he will not get paid the $30,000 dollars he has been promised and owed for the months of work he has done. In his grading business in the past couple of years, he has done work for people who did not pay him and left him with more debts for materials for that job. In other words, he has worked his very hardest and paid the company for which he has worked to work for them. Like so many people during these hard times, he has found it very difficult to trust that people will do what they say they are going to do.

I do what I always do when he calls and began to reassure him that it is going to be okay (that is what he calls me for). Then I realized that I needed to give him the reassurance that I know that God is going to do what He says He is going to do. I know that His love is changeless and that He doesn't break any of His promises.

To reassure Waylon, I ended up telling him about some of my experiences that I had recently being having and that I was going to write this book. Waylon is very busy and most of our conversations are quick ones. He calls when he is just about to be home and has realized he hasn't talked to me in a couple of days or on his way to a job after he has made the calls he has to make to get his workday going.

I am telling you this in order for you to understand how unusual it is for us to have enough time in the middle of his work day to talk for as long as we talked. You see the day before he had to drive an hour and a half down the interstate to pick up trees for a job he was completing. Today, he had had to go that same route to pick up just one more. Coincidence or was God setting up the right time and place for the next step in my life to unfold?

After I got off the phone, I realized that I had not even thought about what it would mean to have to tell people about my experiences. I had not thought twice about writing the book. The Holy Spirit had said to write it, and I started this record of my experiences. Now, I felt as if He had thrown this right in my face, because I was thinking about what people would think about me. I was still not in the stage of my training and learning from *A Course in Miracles* where I did not judge myself or people like the *Course* wanted me to do. I wasn't really prepared to tell people yet. Of course, my son Waylon, if I had had the time to think about it, was the first person I should tell. He had always been my biggest supporter in whatever I tried to do, whether it was get another divorce or furthering my education while working a full time job. Yes, I could depend on Waylon and God.

Once that first conversation about this experience was over with, I found contentment. I knew Waylon supported me (even though I made him promise not to send me to the looney bin). I was just shocked, because I hadn't even thought about having to do tell people. After that conversation though, I found myself elated that my big secret was finally out of the bag.

That night I just lay in bed. It was another one of those nights where I didn't sleep very well. But, this time it was because I was anticipating the next leg of the journey on which the Holy Spirit was going to take me. That physical feeling of my body tingling all over that began when this journey began was still present. I was beginning to get more accustomed to it. I might as well, because it seems to be with me most of the time now. In fact it has been with me for so long now, that I finally am sure that all of the molecules that comprise my body are not going to vibrate against one another fast enough to bounce off one another and send my body in minute particles into space (even though it feels like it some of the time).

As I lay there, that small still quiet voice told me to tell my friends Jeanie, Ann, Danette, Debbie, and Patti next. I was to offer them the opportunity to go on this journey with me. All of these ladies started off as my colleagues. We all worked together teaching at an alternative school. Over the years, that relationship has changed into what it is today. They are my family as well as those with which I am tied to by blood.

During our times as teachers at the alternative school, we have collaborated on many projects. We were always trying to come up with ways to help more of the alternative students that come through our doors be successful in life.

Debbie, Patti, and I went through our doctoral program together. I can't tell you how many presentations we have done together in our classes.

Jeanie is my kindred spirit. We are at the same points in our life, have gone through similar life experiences, and enjoy doing many of the same kind of things with our recreational time. Jeanie and I spent one day a week for an entire summer writing a collaborative syllabus that taught American history and literature utilizing videos.

Danette, is the daughter of my heart. When she went through her divorce, we spent almost every night together when her ex-husband had her kids. Most of these times were at my house sipping wine and talking about everything and anything, but the majority of our conversations centered on how to help our school be the kind to help more young people.

Ann is the daughter I was just beginning to know before my life went in the direction it is going. The last 2 years at the alternative school our jobs as Instructional Lead Teacher and Instructional Technology Specialist put us together doing many different projects and in doing so cemented our relationship to what we have now.

There are other friends in my life that the Holy Spirit could have named, but I am confident that He knows more than I do. And even though their names came to me and I did not want to hurt their feelings, I heard that quiet, still voice guide me and did as I was instructed.

The next morning, I thought about what I had heard in the night and made a plan for getting it done. In the afternoon right before school lets out, I had the time to email Patti and Ann at school to ask them for their home email addresses (I had everyone else's). When I got their email addresses, I pondered what to say to these ladies in the email I would send to their homes.

I did not want any of them to feel as if they were being pressured, and I did not yet know what role they were to play. I just knew that I was to tell my big secret to them next and give them the opportunity to go with me on this journey. I started thinking about them as a whole and as individuals. First of all Patti, Ann, Jeanie, and Danette all teach (Guess what?), you guessed it – English. If you were going to write a book, wouldn't you want the majority of your friends to be experts in literature and grammar? Is that a coincidence? I don't think so! Next, I thought about them as individuals. Jeanie, my feminine soul mate, was a piece of cake. I knew she would be there, even though her life is very full with raising a great granddaughter in her retirement years. Danette's maternal relatives are American Indian, and she is much attuned to her spiritual self. I had already encouraged her in one of our shopping outings of the past to purchase for herself a copy of *A Course in Miracles*. I also was aware that with 3 small kids she had not had an opportunity to study it. But, I was assured she had it and could take the course when the time was right for her and that she would not be surprised about my news. I was sure Patti would understand, as the two of us had discussed wanting to join *A Course in Miracles* study group at some point in time. Debbie is my ground. She is the most down to earth person I know. We have not talked about spiritual things. I know she was raised as a Catholic, but that is pretty much it as far as her religious beliefs go. I really wanted her to be a part of this. No, I needed her to be there. If she could read this, I knew she would give me the "everyday Joe's (or in this case Josephine's)" reaction.

After much contemplation this is what I sent to them in a joint email with an attachment that contained the very beginnings of my thoughts for the book:

Hey my friends,

I know you ladies must wonder why I have been so reclusive, but things have been happening to me which I just am beginning to understand. I haven't understood until now why I do not want to go back to Lake Jackson, why is Jeanie even further away than that, why am I in this area, why I haven't gotten one of the many jobs I have applied for to teach on a ground college campus near here. Well, while I have been here, I have been reading *A Course in Miracles.* I have read it before, but never found the time to complete the lessons which are a type of mind training. Now, I am on lesson 104 out of 364 and some strange things have been happening to me. So, I have a strange request of you ladies. First of all, none of you have to accept this request. Believe me, when I say I will have perfect peace with anyone who does not want to receive any more of these types of correspondences from me. I will always love and treasure each of you as my friends no matter what happens with this. Here it is - I am going to write a book. I have attached the notes that I have begun to write and the very beginnings of my experiences. I love all you ladies and do not think it is a coincidence that 4 of you are English teachers with Debbie there as my grounding force or that we have not collaborated on many other types of projects. I could not sleep last night. My body is vibrating almost all of the time. I can't really explain it, yet I am hoping some of you will be able to help me clarify in words what I am experiencing. And, if you can't or don't want to help with clarification, then maybe it is just support. I know that some people will not understand what I am trying to do, and I will need you to be a sounding board some of the time. I also do not know what your roles will be, but I know I am supposed to offer you the opportunity to share in this journey with me (that is one of the things that I heard last night as I couldn't sleep). I told Waylon this morning, because it was sort of thrust upon me to do it. I have not said another word to anyone else. I made Waylon promise me he would not lock me up in the looney bin. So, ladies I am interested to see what each of you have to say.

Loving all of you for being just who you are,

Tana

Of course, I had to wait. While I was waiting, the ego was saying things like – "I hope they don't think I'm one of those crazy people and start avoiding me when I call or text? and "What if one of them says no?" Then, I would remember that God is love and I was doing what He wanted me to do, so everything was going to be fine.

The first to reply was the one who I was the most unsure about. I was not unsure about what kind of friend she was, because I already knew she was a PHENOMENAL friend (as all of them are). I meant I was not certain about how comfortable she was in taking a spiritual journey with me. I should have known God would appease my anxiousness with her email first. Here is what I saw when I opened her email. By the way, the first lines of this email are her way of saying. "Do you know how unusual it is for me to get this message from you in this way!" **Is God talking to us? Are we listening?**

> Hey,
>
> It is unusual for me to look at my e-mail on a Friday - it's Mexican night you know. Your letter was at the top of my inbox. What a terrific idea - I believe that you have so much to say - and many will benefit from your sharing.
>
> I am proud of you for getting to be okay with yourself. I know that we (me) have all counted on you for your positive outlook and your belief in us.

I know that learning to listen is often easier
said than done - and I will be excited to see
what you do and to be a sounding board!

Love you deary!

dq

Jeanie's was the next to come. Here are her
words:

What to say. The first thing I can think of is
I need to read this book. The next thing is of
course I believe in you and will be there for and
with you in anything u choose to do in any
way I can- the next thing is I want this journey
to be one i take with u and one I can take for
myself (does that make sense?). Call me when
you can and we will talk. Love u much!

Since Jeanie's fulltime duty is her great granddaughter,
I recognized that her words meant we could have an
actual telephone chat at that time (again very unusual).
I called her. We talked for over an hour. I was trying to
give her more in depth knowledge about my experiences.
While we were doing that, I related some of my thoughts
after reading Gary Renard's book *The Disappearance of
the Universe* about his having visitors from another time
appearing to him in his home after practicing the lessons
from *A Course in Miracles*. She knows me pretty well,
so I told how I wanted my spiritual experience to NOT
include visitors here in my bedroom - especially since I
sleep in the nude! That made us both laugh. God wants

this experience to be joyful, and I hope some of you are laughing as you read this (even if it is to my humiliation of telling the whole world about that other secret I've been keeping).

After Jeanie's email and after I had gone to bed, Patti's reply came next into my inbox. Here is what I read the morning of the third day of chronicling my experiences.

> Oh, Tana, how lovely to hear from you. I must say that I am not the least bit surprised by your decision. You have always been, for me, the friend who was willing to go with what you knew was right, even if you didn't know what that was. I am thrilled. I am thrilled that I am one of the names on the list of those you want on this journey with you and I am thrilled that you are embarking on it at all. I can only hope that I will come to some sort of clarity as well. You know I have had similar issues with getting jobs I have applied for. Still don't know what that means for me, but for now I am happy that you are taking the steps you feel are the right ones. I love you dearly and miss you more than I say, or can say. ... I'm proud of you girl, and all you need to do is ask and I'm there for you.
>
> Much love,
>
> Patty

Ann's was next. With her 2 boys and many other responsibilities her email was short and to the point, but nonetheless just as necessary for the nurturing of the human part of this experience for me. Her words were to the point and so appropriate as always. Simply she said, "I love it! I would be honored to help!" Each email I received affirmed God's love through these people that continuously give me their love and support.

On that 3rd morning, I began to do my *Course in Miracles* routine. I got to the part where I was once again going to try and watch the video and hear the message the Master Teacher had for me. You know the one that had been interrupted 2 days in a row. Well during the night, (to be exact it was 3:30 AM) I woke up to this beeping sound.

It sounded like the computer. I started trouble shooting it, because I did not want that beeping sound to wake me up again! I checked and saw that it was plugged in. I opened it up (it had been in sleep mode like I leave it every time with all of my internet Windows ready and for easy access for doing my *A Course* in Miracles "stuff" and the Word document on which I had been writing my ideas about this book), and it had rebooted.

For that quick nanosecond my still untrained mind was thinking, "Stupid McAfee that takes control and loads the updates even when I have not given it permission to do so!" Then, the mind training kicked in and I remembered God is love and He wants peace for me. Gone is the "mad at McAfee feelings" and here is the peace that comes with the realization that God is leading me. I had given him permission to make decisions with me, so I waited patiently this time for everything to reload and started typing words for some part of this book. You needed this part of the story to understand the rest of what happened that morning.

First, I have to search for themasterteacher.tv website. I thought I had made a tab, so I could just click the tab and have the Internet page right in front of me - WRONG. Then, I found it and had to put my user name and password in. It kept saying it was wrong. I finally located my username and password in a notification email. I was finally able to get logged on, find the video, and had begun watching it after trying for 3 days to see it.

I had just gotten past "God's Commercial", and the Master Teacher was trying to help me remember about our past lives together 60 years ago when yes, you guessed it, the phone rang again. The ring tone was not my son's Calypso, and he had told me yesterday that he was determined not to disturb me again after doing so for the past 2 days. I had reassured him that whatever happened, happened and that I was glad to hear from him whenever he had the chance to call.

The ring tone that came from my phone was *All You Need is Love*. That's the one that is set for anyone who does not call me very often. That ring tone is another part of the story.

I had been to Biloxi the week before with my dad and sister to gamble. It is what my "normal" family did with a small amount of money for recreational purposes.

I was trying to train my mind not to worry about money. Most of the time, I had done a good job. I thought that I would win a little money. Wasn't it part of God's abundant blessing without freaking out the ego? Well, I lost my $200 early and had to resort to enjoying watching people for the rest of the trip.

After that, I was downhearted and thinking about whether I was interpreting the course correctly. For some reason that escapes me for now, I went to the BlackBerry Applications website. I had been to that website and many others a few times looking for cool, free ringtones; but had yet to find any. That day, the first link on the web page I went to was a free (yes, free- how often do you find a free ring download for your phone) download for the song *All You Need is Love*. This song is the one I keep hearing in my head when I meditate. It was, I had realized earlier in the course, another way for God to talk to me. So, whenever the phone rings it reassures me that God is love and has a good, better plan than the one I think I want. **Do we think all of this is still just coincidences or is God talking to us?**

Back to the story I was trying to relate to you. By the third day in a row that the phone rings while I am trying to watch the next video, I am very much at peace about not seeing it again today. In fact, I giggled internally. When I answered the phone, I was very surprised (even though now I do not know why I am surprised about anything that is happening to me:-) to hear my brother's voice. My baby brother is 12 years younger than I am, so I am more like his mother than sister. Even today,

I can't remember whether it is my brother or son who had the measles! During these dark, hard times it is no surprise that he, like so many others, is unemployed. He has also been battling depression since his divorce. My mother's passing 3 years previously had sunk him deeper into depression's darkness. He has recently met a wonderful woman, who has brought laughter into his life again along with helping him stay more connected with his family. I am telling you all of this to help you once again realize that my brother calling me is a VERY unusual thing.

He told me he had a dream about all of us, including mom. In his dream we were trying to put mud on a wall. I thought, "Well if you think you have something unusual to tell, just wait to you hear mine!" Then, I laughed and told him about what I was going through. Again, I had not thought about how to tell my brother. And again, the perfect opportunity had arisen. I asked him why he had called me, other than to tell me the dream. He said something just told him to call me. **God, are you talking to us? Are we listening?**

3
Day Four

God, how do I know it is Your Voice talking to me and not the ego's?

Self: God You're right, how could I not notice all of the good things happening to me and my family recently! Which one do You want to talk about first?

Self: Yes, my sister Lynn's back is being healed as we talk. In fact, she is in much less pain than she has been in a very long time, and she almost needs no pain medication. That is a big improvement from the opiate patches she had to wear a few months ago!

Self: And no, I hadn't forgotten that other miracle which has blessed Lynn and our family! It is still hard to believe that after 39 years, she has the peace of having spent time with the daughter she gave up for adoption all those years ago! We are all so excited that Gia is coming into our lives and going to allow us to envelop her in our love! We are all patient now and waiting for the time to be right in the near future where we get to meet her!

Self: Yes God, I remember how hard it has been for me to learn Your lesson and not be worried about money to pay the bills, especially in the difficult times we are having now.

Self: And yes, I know it was You I heard, when Aunt Jean and I went by dad's house at Lake Seminole and saw the realtor's car in the driveway. Didn't I go right in her house and call my dad and tell him someone was looking at the house? You know I wouldn't have gotten his hopes up for nothing, if I wasn't sure I heard Your voice telling me the house was going to sell and that You were taking care of the family's money problems.

Self: You're right God; my son Waylon has so many contracts for grading and landscaping right now, that he told me the other day that he doesn't have to look for more jobs on which to bid. And, all of these contracts are with people who give him assurance that they will pay him.

Self: Don't worry, I haven't forgotten the blessings that my baby brother Jaye is experiencing because of You either. I love watching him smile and laugh again! Last time he was here, he and the new lady in his life were laughing out loud while watching Forest Gump. Carol has helped him find Your joy and extend it to the rest of his family! He is opening up his heart and home to us, again. He even cooks us meals and invites us to come eat! It is a marvelous thing!

Self: You're right, again as always! How can I not know that You are talking to me and the rest of my family when so many miraculous things have occurred in such a short time!

Events of Day 4

Day 4 of putting into words for others to read Tana's journey began with – Yes, I was finally able to see my Master Teacher on that video I had been trying to watch for 3 days now. Finishing it, made me wonder whether I needed to watch another one or not. I wasn't sure what to do, so I didn't watch another one. You see I am at the point in this spiritual journey where I am supposed to let my Guide direct me. Since it is still very new to me, I am not always sure what specific steps I am supposed to take in learning what God wants me to learn next. So today after watching Master Teacher for an hour, I felt like I had spent a long time already and did not want to watch one more spiritual awakening lesson which seemed to be way over my head most of the time. And, I had quite a bit on my mind (can you imagine why).

That previous night, again had been a restless night where I ended getting up and trying to put words to this experience. I mean what else was I supposed to do when I couldn't sleep? I kept thinking about how amazing some of what was happening was unfolding to be! The latest one was the phone call from Jaye. I told you yesterday how unusual it was for him to call, but to call twice in one day! Will wonders never cease? He said he called to get mom's recipe for cooking chicken-and-dumplings (if this had been Paula Deen's story you would have gotten the recipe here-but I am NOT Paula), and I am sure that was part of the reason he phoned. But, he had other mystical experiences which had happened to him that he wanted to relate to me. He said that the previous night when I had been awake at 3:30, that he also woke up and saw a great flash of light. He got up and realized that the light that he leaves on in the kitchen above the sink was out. The next morning he thought it might be the light bulb that caused the previous night's black out, so he took the bulb out to see if it was bad. He looked at it and realized the filament was not broken. While he was looking at it, he dropped it. Not once, but twice. The bulb should have been broken, yet it wasn't. Since it wasn't the bulb, he went and checked the breaker next. He found that it had been tripped, so he reset it. He went back and put that same bulb in the socket and guess what – it worked. He couldn't explain why the light had gone out much less came back on with a bulb that had been dropped twice.

And, that was not the only thing that was strange that night. He and Carol had watched the *Hope for Haiti* TV fund raising. He heard the song *Lean on Me* being sung. During that night he saw in his mind's eye exactly where his fingers should go on a keyboard to play that song. Now, this isn't so strange, except that my brother cannot, nor has he ever played a keyboard. He is very musically inclined and plays a guitar very well. He also is the sound technician for a local band, but that was as far as his musical talent went. It certainly had never extended to a piano. My parents had never even owned one. He said to me, "Tana, I know if I had a keyboard in front of me now that I could play *Lean on Me*!"

One of these occurrences is not so weird, but ALL of these say to me that this many strange things at one time are NOT coincidences! **God are we hearing Your Voice?**

The coolest part of all of this for me, is that I realized that Jaye is going to be my "mystical experiences" comrade on this journey. It has been very difficult for me, not to have anyone close that truly understands this part of the journey. Is it a coincidence that right now he is unemployed and has the time to stay awake and experience strange things and then talk to his sister about it? Again, I don't believe in this many coincidences!

Today was also the day that I began to have a few doubts. I mean who was I kidding; who would want to read my book, much less buy it? I had sent out drafts to my friends, yet had not heard anything from anyone. Of course, right after those doubts entered my mind, emails flew into my inbox. Carol, the special woman in my brother's life, was first. She wrote:

> Tana if you could see how hard of a time
> that Jaye and I are having opening up the
> attachments that you are sending. I'm sure
> you would laugh as we have while trying to
> do this…..Just wanted you to know that I

can't wait to open my email each day to read
the next installment from the next bestselling
author Tana Tillman, the sister that I've always
wanted and now I have!!!! Love you lots and
keep up the good work!!!!!

Carol's email brought tears of joy to my eyes! She
and my brother anxiously awaited each future draft!
How could I doubt what God had inspired and would
continue to inspire me to do?

I knew I had to let Carol know how much her email
touched my heart, so I replied:

Carol my sister,

I am now calling you the shortened version of
the name Jaye calls you. I have an Aunt Jean
and now I have sister Carol…

I am so glad that you chose to write yourself
into my story (as you should) and take the
place in it where you belong as my sister.

You will never know how much your email
meant to me - 1- because I am so excited about
the story and I haven't had any more feedback
about it since initial support. So, your and
Jaye's enthusiasm to read the next installment
assures me that people will want to read it.

Secondly, you joined with me in seeing myself
as the famous author. You know the verse
that says "Where 2 or more or gathered in my

name". Today, it means a whole new thing to me. I used to think it should make me feel guilty about not being in a church on a Sunday like today. But, not this one. Today the verse says to me that when 2 minds aligned with God see the same things to honor His name, then He will make them happen! Thank you for blessing me with that thought!...

Okay I have another idea to get started with and want to put some of it down before I go get dressed for dad and I to go out to eat!

Love you,

Sis

And the emails kept coming! Jeanie's was short, but gladdened my heart with the reassurance in the short amount of time she has she was reading my drafts, anticipating the next one, and taking the time to tell me all that in an email.

Next was Patti's. She said it made her giggle (YEAH!) and want to read what came next. She felt like I made it easy to understand. Ann's email followed Patti's closely in both the time it arrived in my inbox and the message she wanted to convey. I was joyful in the evidence my family and friends had provided! I would be able to reach people with the message God wanted me to convey!

As Day 4 progressed, I was beginning to think I wouldn't have anything to tell you about it. I didn't think that I could provide you with anymore evidence of the astounding experiences God was allowing me to have! Again, boy was I wrong! I still can't quite get used to all of this!

Sometime in that morning, I got the beginnings of a headache. I have food allergies that cause me to get them if I don't avoid those foods I'm allergic to, so I did not think much about it. I just went and took Tylenol. I tried to remember what I had eaten the previous day in order to avoid that food for a few days. Did I have any chocolate? No, I left off the CarbSmart ice cream yesterday. What about nuts? No, I hadn't eaten any. In other words, I went through the entire list of foods to which I am allergic and could not identify the cause of this particular headache.

Also another strange thing about this one is that after an hour, the Tylenol did not take the pounding in my head away. In fact, it was one of the worst ones I had had in a long time. I just didn't understand it. I had recited *A Course in Miracles Rules for Decisions* many times along with the rule for correction. None of this worked! I just didn't understand it. God had blessed me with all of these wonderful things, and I believe He will continue to do this. Then, why did I feel so lousy?

Okay, are you ready for the supernatural stuff? I had been out to eat with my dad. I came home and went upstairs to my room. My computer is sitting on the floor beside my chair. Do you remember me telling you that I keep all of my tabs for me to do my *A Course in Miracles* routine and the Word doc on which I am working up and ready to access? Well, again my computer made a strange noise. I bent over and picked it up. A popup from one of my Dell programs came up. It wanted me to pick my Avatar. Now, I hadn't asked that to appear! So, I closed that particular window down. All of the sudden, the screen went dark. Those white letters came up that said it was going to do a memory dump and shut down to prevent further damage! I tried to do what the *A Course in Miracles* tells me to do and stay at peace. Now, that is NOT easy when you are trying to write a book and having to start a new online class the next day. For a second I panicked and began to ask myself if I had saved the latest book doc and where was I going to get another computer by tomorrow to teach online. I dug deep and drug up a little peace. To keep the little peace I had found, I didn't watch the computer take all that time to reload. I really tried to pretend that the computer wasn't deciding whether it was ever going to work again or not. I just kept saying to myself that God was going to take care of it.

All of the sudden, the music that precedes The Master Teacher's broadcast came floating to my ears. The broadcast was playing! You know the one! It was the one from that morning; the one I couldn't decide to watch or not. I thought, "Tana, I guess you are supposed to watch it, and it needs to be now!" So, I leaned over and picked up the computer. My head was killing me, yet I figured if God went to that much trouble to get me to watch it, then I better watch it- headache or not.

Of course, what do you think the video was about? Yes, you got it! It was about healing. I kept watching and thinking I was going to have a GREAT story to tell you about my instantaneous healing. Well, afraid not. It did ease off, and as soon as the video ended I went and got more Tylenol. Right now, it is completely gone. Maybe instantaneous healing would have frightened the ego. I still don't get all of this, but I keep trying!

Evidently the message Master Teacher was trying to get me to learn is a very difficult one for my mind to learn, or I am taking it way too literally! I think I understand the basic premise of the lesson. I think he is telling me that the ego thinks it has left God and His complete Oneness. Because it does think that, the ego thinks it deserves punishment such as death, suffering and pain. Master Teacher says that we have never really left God, so we need to let the thoughts of killing God and His Oneness by separation go from our mind. He says that it is not true! Master Teacher continually tells me, that God and His children can NEVER be separated; all of this that we think we experience is just dreams we have made up. Since, my head still hurt after watching it for 2 hours, I guess we'll be working on really getting this lesson again in the near future! I guess you'll just have to read the next stage of the story to find out if Tana learns these lessons or not! **God, am I hearing Your Voice?**

4
Days Five and Six

God, you want me to tell them WHAT?

Self: God, You've got to be kidding me, right? You can't expect me to tell them that! They're not going to believe it! They haven't had the prep work You've done with me to really know that it is You talking to them! They're not going to believe me! They're gonna think I'm, some sort of kook! I mean, I've heard the mix of Bible verses and *A Course in Miracles* You've had me read. And, I've heard Master Teacher keep reminding me all the time that Jesus is here with us, but Lord they haven't!

Self: You're right God; I know I'm not the only one that gets frightened when they think about the whole time thing. I mean just recently dad and Waylon were discussing how it frightened them and those manly, men of mine NEVER talk about their fears - especially those that have to do with things like that! But, God.

Self: Okay, so you want me to say that all of our lives are like a film strip. That as individuals each of us is sitting in our own projection booth with our own films that each of us has created, and playing them, and deciding what the others in our own movie are saying. And, that how do we know what the other characters are saying when they're not actually there, because they're each in their own projection booth watching the one they created for their individual self making up what the characters in their movie of life are saying. But wait, how does somebody else know what I would say in their movie?

Self: Oh, they don't know what I would say. So, you say that each of us has forgotten that we are Your perfect children and that we never really have left our home with You? And, each of us has just decided we could be separated from Your One True Source of Love? But God, can we ever be really separated from you?

Self: Oh, good. You had me scared for a minute! I mean I can't imagine my life without You in it! So, back to explaining that time thing. What do you want me to say next?

Self: Okay, our life is like that film. We keep putting it on the reel and playing it over and over again. We take it off and change the script, and we keep watching it over and over again. So You're saying that, if in our own film we recognize that all the other characters in our film are not really there because they're in their own projection booth and we don't judge them (make up what they would say or do when they are NOT really in our film of our individual life) because we know that each of us are really Your perfect children created in Your own image, that we can get out of this "trapped in time" cycle and come Home. How do we get out of this film about a life that is full of pain, suffering, and death and wake up from it back in our true home?

Self: All right. Let me see if I got this right. You said that whenever anyone does anything or says anything that we don't like we just do nothing! But, what if they are cussing me out?

Self: Oh, that's right we made that script for him to say up. They're in their projection booth making up what I'm saying while I'm in mine making up what they're saying. Boy, that's convoluted! So, what do I do?

Self: You want me to do nothing! You can't mean it! You must want me to do something!

Self: So, I'm to be still a moment and remind myself that that person I think I'm physically with is really not there and remind myself that really he or she is one of Your perfect children. Then giving that moment of time to You and NOT reacting allows my real, higher self (which I am not aware of) to collaborate with You and Your other children and write a real script where all of us get to say what we really would say in the movie of our REAL life? And, each time we do that, that part of each of our individual film strips where we suffer, experience pain, and die gets cut out of our individual film until our filmstrip in time is gone and the only thing that is playing is the collaborative one that we made with God where we are at home with you where there is not ever in pain, suffering, or death? Man that sounds like HEAVEN! Is that enough for tonight?

Self: Okay God, but before I go back to sleep, I want to give you a couple of shout outs.

Self: Yeah, the first one is for letting me get a few hours of sleep before you compelled me to get up and have to start typing. I really liked getting to bed a little earlier last night. I'm not really sure about the waking up every hour thing though. You wouldn't really understand this physical girl thing, but ever since I got this bladder tack-up I don't know if I have to go to the bathroom or not, so I've got to get up and go try every time you wake me up. Just to make sure. So, will you think about that before you plan for tomorrow night's session? And another thing. Remember that today I have to start going online and typing conversations with my new class of students. You know I've been on a short hiatus between classes while we've been doing this writing everything down stage of our journey, but it ends tomorrow. Just thought you might want to keep those things in mind before we begin again tomorrow.

Self: Oh, yeah the other thing I wanted to thank you for was mixing up the music! I really am about to get tired of hearing the Beatles sing, "All you need is love (bah, bah, bah, bah, bah). All you need is love (bah, bah, bah, bah, bah). All you need is love, love. Love is all you need).” I mean I like them okay, but they were never my favorite group.

Self: You're right God; you did send me, an oldie. I don't remember who sang, “I can see clearly now the rain is gone. I can see all obstacles in my way… It's gonna be a bright, bright sun shiney day. Look all around you there's nothing but blue skies.”

Self: Why did you leave out part of that song? You know I've never been good at hearing the words to a song, much less remembering them.

Self: Oh, the part you left out didn't contain part of the message you wanted me to hear. Okay. I **really** wanted to thank you for my hearing Carrie Underwood (she's one of my favorites) singing, “I told you so. One day you'd wanna come back home…” You know, I used to not like country music. That was before I had to listen to it every time I got in the truck with Waylon when we went somewhere and hearing it in Debbie's truck on our way to Sarasota to go to class. I mean after hours of hearing it you might as well learn to like it! Anyway I thought before we closed our conversation for tonight, that I would thank you for changing up the music you are playing in my head. Good night.

Events of Days 5 & 6

Okay, so that none of you have to stop and go look up who sang the song that begins, "I can see clearly now the rain is gone", I am going to start this day's events a little backwards to answer that question and also show you how God's plan is always easier and better!

Later in the afternoon of Day 5 of my spiritual journey, I got Debbie's (my grounding force) first email since her initial consent to travel on this leg of the journey with me. Wait, let me back up and say that when I typed that song up there without an artist I thought, "Since I don't have an artist, have I got to stop and look it up? No, not now. It is too important to get these words down. I'll just wait until later and see what to do about it."

Now, let's go back to Debbie's email. Of course being the wonderful, supportive friend that she is, she gave me heartfelt words of encouragement. And, then she wrote–

> "I can see clearly now " was one of those songs I always sang as a teenager - I couldn't remember who sang it - James Nash. How often do the lyrics of the old songs bring out or up some of the memories or old feelings?

> Now hold on, for those of you who already knew who the artist was and have started correcting my friend, right behind that email came this one –

> Hey - it's Johnny not James - but you probably already looked that up!

> dq

No, I had not taken the time to look it up, nor had I had to (evidently that's what I have God and friends for). I am beginning to have the "peace that passeth all understanding" when it comes to scurrying around and trying to get all the things that I think I have to get done, done! And, as you can see throughout this book God demonstrates that His plan is much, much better and easier!

Having and maintaining the "peace that passeth all understanding" is a good segue into how the beginning of Day 5 started. I have to admit to you that physically getting the first four days of this journey down so you could read it at the Holy Spirit's pace has been physically draining, though spiritually I'm about as revved up as any one person could be! My eyes have had it! I haven't looked at a computer screen so much since I wrote my dissertation!

Since I was feeling so tired, when I closed up my computer about 4:30 this morning I thought before I went to sleep, "I sure hope that nothing so strange as my computer restarting and MT (I'm tired of typing Master Teacher, so from here on out it's going to be MT) making me sit down and learn my spiritual lessons occurs today. I certainly would like to take a day off from feeling compelled to write it down before I forget the details!"

Imagine my surprise… no wait, Tana (I said to myself) that is not the way you think about it now. Let me start over. When I woke up the next morning I had a warm, reassuring peaceful feeling knowing that today was going to be a day of rest for me. Hmmm, if you put a Day 0 where I was spiritually working diligently with the Holy Spirit to get the beginnings of this book in my higher conscience so that my conscious mind could get started on Day 1 of this book, then this is the 7th day which I think God would want this to be my day of rest on my spiritual journey. **Again, coincidence or is God talking to me?** You have to decide for yourself, because I KNOW the answer to that question.

So, I have not picked up my computer to write anything for more than 24 hours. I woke up and lay in bed and used *A Course in Miracles' Rules for Decisions* as I always do and thought, "I want to have a peaceful, joyful day that is filled with abundant blessings and a healthy, pain free body. If I make no decisions by myself, then this is the day that will be given to me." After that I did my lesson for mind training from *A Course in Miracles.*

I did not watch MT today. I was perfectly at peace that today the computer would not restart for me to be required to hear MT. For one thing, I have finished the series that was under the section titled *The New Beginning.* Yesterday after I finished that set to get the tab ready for tomorrow, I went to the list of videos on MT's website trying to figure out what my Guide was directing me to do next. I looked at all of the series of videos. The sets of videos are not numbered, but each set has a title, and the sets are grouped into a Volume. In fact the videos from Volume III are listed above the links for Volume II, and Volume I. I do not know whether it is like a test to see if you're spiritually advanced enough to figure it out or what. In other words, I still do not get everything that is happening to me! Anyway, when I went to the website I chose Volume I, *The New Beginning*. In my logical mind, I thought it made sense to choose the first volume and the set of videos whose link was at the top, left of the screen. When I went back to the list of sets of videos under Volume I to try and choose the next set that my Guide wanted me to watch, I saw on the top, right the set titled *The Quantum Resolution* and underneath *The New Beginning* was a set titled *This is The Manual For Teachers*. I couldn't decide whether I was supposed to go top, right or second set on the left. I might as well be like the characters in Dan Brown's *The Da Vinci Code* searching for The Holy Grail! To tell you the truth, the thoughts of trying to understand MT when he is talking about all that scientific theory and how it is evidence of what *A Course in Miracles* is saying that what Jesus is saying is true, is more than a little overwhelming to me right now. And I sure am not ready to say I am ready for *The Manual For Teachers*, because even though I taught public school for 33 years I know THAT is not the kind of teacher this is talking about. To make a long story short, I was at peace that today I did not have to spend time watching MT.

"So if I'm not going to write today, what am I supposed to do on my journey to spiritual awakening" I asked myself. I was not sure. I had already completed building a new online education class I was starting to teach, when I started wondering this. I knew one of the reasons I was given time off from the intense time with The Holy Spirit was to spend more time being the ordinary human that I am. I mean, who would want to read a book about being a human who isn't wholly aware of the availability of The Holy Spirit unless I go out and have more experiences as one who is not continually listening to Him.

Well just about then, I heard Calypso on my phone. You know what that means. Waylon is calling. I hadn't heard from him in a couple of days. I thought that was strange, since we were enjoying talking about our embarking on this new journey. After he inquired about me, I asked about how he was doing. He told me that the reason he hadn't called was that he had been in bed for 2 days with the strep throat his wife, Dana had the week before. I asked him if he had been to the doctor. As money is short for his family right now, he had not. I suggested that if he wanted to make money, he needed to be well and that usually strep does not go away on its own. We conversed a few more minutes, and I knew he had to work, so we ended our conversation with his assurance (because he knew as his mom it was my duty to be concerned about how he was feeling) he would talk to me later that day.

After he got off the phone, I gave up to The Holy Spirit a picture of Waylon's body in complete health, as I had been instructed to do in my *A Course in Miracles* training. At this point I do not know how effective this is. Not because of the doubt in what God can do, but because of the power of the ego to not let me write that script of my life with God and without the ego. If I do, then the ego is gone and it fights hard to not let itself die. To appease the ego and have it not fight so hard to keep me in its clutches, I was glad to believe in the magic of doctors and modern medicine in my life's script today. Later in the day Waylon called. After enduring 2 shots, one in each cheek, he felt much better. And, so did I!

"What now," I asked myself. A voice kept telling me to call my brother, which I finally listened to and made the phone call. I am not going to tell you what we talked about. I am going to keep it a secret. But, when I say later on in the book to go back and look at Day 5's chronicle, you'll know what I'm talking about. I mean what book doesn't need some surprises to come in it?

We did have the best hour long (yeah, I'm talking about Jaye) conversation we've had as adults! We'd had quite a few over the past years that were that intense, but those intense conversations were about my trying to convince him that he didn't have to stay in that dark hole of depression in which he spent way too much time.

I haven't told you about how blessed we are to have Jaye still here with us, have I? When Jaye was a younger man and newly married with an infant son and another one expected, he contracted some sort of virus. The medical community never identified it, but it was similar they said to Legionnaire's Disease. He was in the local hospital for about a week, where they tried to diagnose and treat his illness. When the lungs began to shut down along with the liver, they transported him to Tallahassee Memorial Hospital. At that point my sister, Lynn and I were called. I did not think twice (where I usually would-but you don't think in situations like this as you know) about leaving my students with a substitute and no long term lesson plans made. We made the 6 hour drive from Atlanta suburbs in much less than that time. Once we got there, the doctor's news was grave. They did not give us much hope for his living. He was in a room in a special ICU for contagious diseases. We were pretty isolated (I wonder why, duh). His wife who was very pregnant would come, but we would have to go to another waiting room away from the one near my brother's room. She had to bring their oldest son, Patrick with her. I remember being able to watch Patrick learn to crawl in that waiting room, while his wife went to see Jaye. It was almost an hour and a half drive from Lake Seminole where mom and dad and Jaye's family lived. All of us decided that it was best for the health and safety of Jaye's immediate family that his pregnant wife and son remain at home. Mom, dad, Lynn, and I would stay in Tallahassee and keep vigil.

We were blessed to have friends that opened up their home to us. During the day all of us would wait in the waiting room to not miss a chance to talk to one of the doctors and until the next visiting session with Jaye would occur. We split the night up. One night mom and dad would go to sleep at the friend's house and the next time Lynn and I would. We did not want to leave Jaye alone. This pattern went on for a week. We would always be elated when the doctors would come in and say, "The good news is, he made it through another night." They knew it was a virus and even though it was unknown, they knew only Jaye's body could heal it.

During this entire ordeal, dad was the strong one. Every time he could, he would sit by Jaye's hospital bed and say to him things like, "Jaye, picture yourself next year at your home. Patrick is running around and your new son is crawling." He knew the power of positive thoughts and always kept them in the forefront of Jaye's mind even when it appeared he was too sick to hear. Many prayers were sent out asking for his health. We just could not see our lives without him in it! I never will forget the elation we all felt the day the doctors came out and told us he was out of danger. Organs had stopped shutting down, and he was on the mend!

You can see, why I REALLY am JOYFUL to be able to have a 1 hour conversation with my brother!

Since I'm talking about siblings and today is the day she decided to write herself into more of an active role in this story, I need to tell you a little more about Lynn. You remember I told you about how mother almost died when she was born and how she lived with Cousin Maggie. At the time I didn't go into much detail, except to tell you Maggie was childless and spoiled her. The family story goes that Maggie carried Lynn on her hip the entire 3 months she had her and let her sleep in the bed with her and her husband Bill. Can you imagine what it must have been like for Lynn, when she was taken from that environment and brought into one where she knew nobody (especially with what we now know about infant bonding)?

Dad was the parent who believed in spare the rod, then spoil the child. His interpretation of that axiom is that if an infant was not hungry, wet, or ill, then the child should not be picked up out of the crib, and mother was too sick to do much more and take care of a 2 year old on top of caring for an infant. I can't imagine how Lynn felt! No wonder she asked me all the time when we were little, "Are you sure I'm not adopted?" I would always reply, "No, you are NOT adopted!" I can't tell you how many times she asked that same question. As a child, I didn't understand her feelings. I felt perfectly comfortable! As an adult who had not known that both of us had been apart for 3 months from mom and dad during this time, it now makes so much sense.

This is just to help you understand why Lynn and I shared more than the average sibling rivalry. She thought she was adopted, and I couldn't understand why in the world she kept asking me that question! She will tell you she was mean to me. In fact, Uncle Albert (Maggie's dad) and Francis (Maggie's first cousin on her mother's side) nicknamed her "Imp", if that is any indication of her personality. Lynn's favorite form of torture was to pick a fight with me. When she would pick a fight I would think, "If I fight back then we're going to get a whipping for fighting, and if I don't fight back dad is going to whip me for not taking up for myself." I always felt, "Damned if I do, damned if I don't." Lynn said she didn't care if she got a whipping, she was just trying to increase the chances of me getting one.

And on top of all that I had to be, as Lynn always said, "perfect". First of all, I pleased my parents and teachers because I'm a rule follower. Always have been and always will be. I mean, who wouldn't be if the anxiety level of breaking a rule became so high that you thought you were going to have a heart attack! And then, I was a good student. Didn't have to study a whole lot, I just had to pay attention in class (which I did). I used all my time wisely, so I got most of my homework done in class. I also had the speed reading thing (in which dad trained me) going for me.

Lynn, on the other hand, does not like to follow the rules. Why should she? If she did that, then all of the possibilities of what life could bring her were stamped down. Instead she experiences and creates more of life's potential. I do not know today, if she even realizes that while she was envious of my "perfection" I was jealous of her ability to live life to its fullest and not be afraid to try things that haven't been tried.

Lynn, on top of all that, as an adult has been diagnosed as having Attention Deficient Disorder (ADD). Basically, that means that the brain does not function as it should for focusing and it would not let her pay the attention to which she needed to retain the concepts and to be a successful student in school especially in the way they were set up then. In other words, she did GREAT in Home Ec, PE, and Music. She did awful in history, math, and English. She tells me all the time that she wishes she could have been a student in an alternative school like the one at which I taught. She could have watched movies and understood the themes, created a poster about it and been an all "A" student. If only all students could feel success! Oh, wait a minute! That's another book in a whole different venue!

Do you get the picture about our relationship? Do you see why sending her the email about my writing this book brought the most apprehension to me? It wasn't a whole lot of apprehension, because I really knew God was telling me the entire time that my sister loves and supports me in all I do. It is just that doggoned ego! Its voice is pretty quiet now, but every now and then it takes an opportunity to throw up something from my past like Lynn's and my relationship to tell me that what I have done in the past makes me a prime candidate for God not to bless me and for Him to judge me as sinful. But, I showed that old ego! I waited patiently for Lynn to email me back with her offer of support. I had to wait 3 days. Here's how my conversation with God and my ego went.

Self: Okay, God you want me to send Lynn an email about You're telling me to write a book? What makes You think now is the time? I thought we were going to wait until she got here in a few days where I could explain it in person.

Self: Yes you're right; she is on her computer checking her email now. We know that because she just sent me the sweetest message about sisters and the love they share. And again, I can see the benefit of You having time with her to help her understand what is happening better than I can. So, I'm sending it right now.

1 day after the email was sent

Ego: Lynn has had your email for a whole day and hasn't responded to it yet. You know right now she's thinking you are CRAAAZZZY!

Self: God told me he was taking care of it and that she loves and supports me along with Him, so I'm going to ignore you!

2 days after the email was sent

Ego: Can you ignore me today? It's been 2 days now and she hasn't responded. Well, I think if your God loves you so much, He wouldn't make you keep waiting and doubting your sister's love. That's what I think!

Self: God, has kept His promises to me and sent me abundant blessings. I know he hasn't forgotten me and the promises He made. You can't even begin to imagine the kind of love God has for me!

3 days after the email was sent

Ego: Well are you ready to listen to me now? You know your sister never goes 3 days without checking her email. You know she's read it, thinks you have lost it, and has NO clue what to respond with! Where is your God now?

Self: Get behind me Satan! Look at the email my sister sent me!

> Well one of us had to tell the story no matter
> how strange it seems. Glad you stepped up
> to the plate, now I'll support and help you all

I can. Can't wait to see you tomorrow. Just
opened my computer for the first time this
weekend. My back feels good again.
love your sister

Self: Where are you now, Ego? I CAAANNN'T hear
you.

Ego:

Self: That's what I thought! You have no power in the
face of God's love and amazing grace!

Not only was Lynn supportive, but she came to our
house to spend time with me and dad and to talk about
this book. Do you remember earlier I said that we had
been blessed this year with Lynn getting to meet Gia,
the daughter she gave up for adoption 39 years ago? Her
first news for us after she arrived was that Gia had invited
her to attend her son's birthday in a few weeks. Lynn
was going to get to meet the grandchildren that she did
not even know existed a few months previously! Can you
imagine the joy that filled our hearts with her news!

Now, do you know what's coming next? Yes, another
one of those weird things that keep happening to my
family. When Gia made contact with Lynn for the first
time a few months ago (they had found each other
through a web site 10 years ago and only had a few
emails after the initial contact), she told Lynn that she
had a son, Jake, and a daughter, Maya. What's strange
about that? Unbeknownst to Gia, her birth grandparents'
names were Jack and Myra! Do you think it is just
another coincidence that Gia named her children names

that are just one letter different than my parents? None of us think so! The rest of the family can't wait to see the pictures Lynn will bring back from Jake's 5th birthday party and know that it is just a little while until the rest of the family will get to take "brag" picture of our own!

God, I hear the promises you make to me and I am a joyful witness to all your bountiful blessings!

Part 2

A Leap of Faith

5
Week Two

God, how do I overcome the lure of the ego's voice and listen only to You?

Self: God, now you want me to do what!

Self: I can't believe you think I should be Your messenger and tell particular people what You are saying to them!

Self: God, I really have no problems doing what You ask me to do when it involves just me, but now you are asking me to tell them to do things that involve their futures including their money!

Self: God You're right, I have accepted this role as being one of you messengers by writing this book, so I guess telling particular people what you're saying in an email is not much different than that.

Self: Okay God, first you want me to tell Waylon that he is to name the center we are going to build *The New Beginnings Inspiration Center*.

Self: But God, the center was Waylon's idea.

Self: You're right God; it was really Yours. It is not an easy lesson to look at all people as your children, created in Your image when we think we witness the terrible things they seem to do. It is so difficult to believe that this life is not real, but yet a hologram we have created where we are separate from You which You keep reminding me could NEVER happened!

Self: But wait, I told him yesterday that he could plan and name the center. In fact when he was talking about all of his ideas I began to feeling so overwhelmed that I wanted him to stop talking about it! It was difficult in that moment to feel the peace You have promised me!

Self: You're right, again as always! Part of my journey is to hear Your voice through the people You have sent me, so that each of us can be each other's helpmates.

Self: God, you want me to tell my friend to do what!

Self: So God, let me see if I've got this right. You want me to tell her to sell her house! But God that is downright meddling in her life and the market to sell houses right now is TERRIBLE! And you know what else; now this is something you have no clue about. It's awful to have to go to work 5 days a week and before you leave your house you have to make sure EVERYTHIING is perfect in it, because a realtor might show your house on the day you left your bed unmade. I mean, what if you had to physically work so hard to keep your house that clean!

Self: Okay God I'll do what you say. I know it is not me telling her, it's just me giving Your message in order for her to have an opportunity that you think is right for her. But, it is sure going to feel strange telling her this. So what's next on your "to do" list for me?

Self: No not that! I mean telling one friend to do something for which she has the potential to make money pretty quickly I can see the benefits of, but that is very different from telling a friend to invest $80,000 in a piece of property that is in a place for which she has never expressed any interest and that's a LOT of money for one of us middle class folks to invest!

Self: You're right God; You haven't steered me wrong. I will do it. But again, there is a good chance that they're really going to think I've lost it! I really don't want them to start avoiding me for butting into their business! All I want to know, Father, did my older brother, Jesus, experience as much angst as I am experiencing now when you told him to tell the disciples to leave their lives and come follow him?

Self: Okay God, this one is easy. I don't mind writing part of my brother's future story for this book and sending it to him to show him Your assurance that you have good things planned for him.

Self: Before we end this conversation, I want to take this opportunity once again to thank you for mixing up the music even more which you send to my head. I don't miss not hearing *All You Need is Love* one bit. I also think it's really cool that you are sending them to me even when we're not talking!

Self: The first one you sent when I wasn't meditating made me giggle with joy that I was hearing you even when I wasn't consciously thinking about you, and it was so appropriate! There I was getting ready to brush my teeth. I noticed the blue light on the toothbrush charger and the one from the night light, and all of the sudden a song that I haven't thought of in a half a century popped into my head! I heard in my head, "This little light of mine, I'm going to let it shine. This little light of mine, I'm going to let it shine. This little light of mine, I'm going to let it shine. Let it shine. Let it shine. Let it shine." I certainly got the message that you are reassuring me that writing this book is what you want me to do, so thank you. I certainly enjoy our times together. I can't wait to talk to you again!

Events of Week 2

Well, today's tale begins the next stage of my journey! I can tell it's the next stage, because my lessons that I do each morning from *A Course in Miracles* are so appropriate each day that I have tears of joy flowing down my face when I read it and my body is vibrating at a much higher level. Each and every day I am filled with anticipation to see what unfolds next in my life's story! There are so many WONDERFUL things happening in my life now that I can't keep them straight in my head time wise! Because of that, I'm now going to tell you about each week of this journey instead of each day (whew, it was becoming very difficult to keep up with each day).

Where to begin? To help you understand that I AM getting God's lesson on listening to other people, I guess I'll start with what happened first this week that reinforced His lesson. My sister, Lynn, is here with dad and me at our coastal house visiting this week (YEAH). We went on a girl's shopping spree for the house. You know, trying to find those special touches to mix all the old stuff from our parent's house into our new vision of what this one should look like with the least amount of money possible. But, first we had to do lunch! We went to my sister's favorite place to have shrimp quesadillas. While we were waiting on our food, Lynn looked down at mom's wedding ring that I wear. She said that I ought to take it apart and wear the 3 bands separately. You see the ring was a compilation she created out of her wedding band and some diamonds and rubies she had inherited from her cousin, Maggie. You know, the one who kept Lynn as a newborn. I had always thought that mother's wedding band surrounded on top and bottom by another band of rubies and diamonds was too wide. I thought about it for just a second. I realized that God had spoken to Lynn, and Lynn was relaying His information. Not only had I not liked the 3 bands together, but Cousin Maggie had pierced my ears when I was a teen. She had gotten me to do it by promising me her ruby earrings. When she passed, unfortunately, that promise was not fulfilled. You see, someone that had stayed in the home to help nurse her in her last stages of cancer had taken all of her nice jewelry. I told Lynn that was a good idea, but I thought I would make each of the diamond and ruby bands into earrings. The diamonds and rubies had come from Maggie, so now I would have the earrings she always promised me.

Oh, I forgot to tell you about Alice. I had asked Lynn to drive to the restaurant, because I wanted to talk to Alice. You see, two days previously Alice's name came to my head. Yesterday my dad said, "Tana, have you told Mary Alice about the book yet? You know she writes an inspirational, humorous piece for her local paper each month. I think you need to tell her." I sort of snapped back at dad, "Yes, I know I need to tell Alice." Now, I wasn't mad with dad. I was impatient with myself for receiving God's message to tell Alice and not having done anything about it yet! Feeling guilty about the tone of my words I had used with my dad I added, "Dad, when you talk to Bill (dad's nephew), ask him for Alice's (Bill's wife) home email address."

I knew Bill was going to call dad, because he and Alice were planning on coming to see us soon. Just a little while later Bill did call, and dad did ask him for Alice's email address. He was unable to give it to us, as Alice had recently changed it. He said he would have Alice call me. When he said that, I just figured God wanted me to talk to Alice first instead of getting an email. No big deal!

A little later, Waylon called and said Alice didn't have my new number and had called him and told him to tell me to call her (whew!). He asked if I had something to write the number on. I went over to my bedside table and picked up a piece of paper and wrote Alice's number on it. When I got off the phone with Waylon, I turned over the used envelope on which I had written the number. I know my eyes were wide with surprise when I asked my sister, "Guess what is on the other side of this envelope!" She replied without hesitation, "Mary Alice's address." See, now even my sister is not the least bit surprised when God sends us signs that we are doing what He has asked us to do! Here I was thinking I was keeping the Christmas cards on my bedside table to make sure I had everybody's address for next year when I sent them out, but God put it there to assure me that His love is great!

Let's get back to our eating lunch. On the way to the restaurant, I called Alice. I got her at work, so our conversation was short. I told her about the book and that I wanted to send her a copy. She said, "Great!" I told her about writing her phone number on the back of the envelope on which she had sent the Christmas card, and she laughed. We made plans to talk more the next weekend when she and Bill got here.

Okay, now let's go back to the shopping trip! When I tell all you people who love to shop what happens next, now don't go getting into your heads that you will always have "good shopping karma (that's what the daughter of my heart, Danette calls her gift)" if you listen to God's voice. It only happens that way, I believe, when He has a lesson for you to learn or a blessing He wants you to receive.

Lynn and I went into the store looking for a new spread to put on an inherited, antique youth bed which we had decided needed to sit in the corner of the great room of our coastal home, just as it had in our parent's house on Lake Seminole. The coastal home's great room was more modern, so we were looking for something to tie the old with the new. When we walked in the door, I found a memory foam mattress topper for Lynn who had laid on mine that I had gotten just recently to make my older mattress more comfortable. She had said when she laid on mine that it made her bad back feel a little better. Now what are the chances that I would see on the clearance rack right in front of the door only one box of memory foam mattress topper that was a half inch thicker than mine and $20 cheaper than the one I had bought and it was the full size that she needed! I mean I could see it as a coincidence if there had been a queen, twin, and/ or king; but only one and it was exactly perfect! Come on, that is NOT a coincidence! We knew it was put there just for Lynn, so we put it in our buggy.

On to our next find! We pushed the buggy around the store to the bedspread section to look for the spread. The minute we got into that section, our eyes went to the spread on one of the display beds. It was the exact one we had spent hours searching for and ordering online for Lynn's bedroom! We had resorted to shopping online, because there had not been a wide enough selection in the stores. We had already looked at numerous stores. You know what we mean. We were at the coast, now. We wanted a coastal theme. The room was painted blue, so it had to have blue and other calming colors. We had walked down aisles in so many stores. Our feet and backs had ached from searching to find just the perfect one. But now in front of us was a wide selection of that exact "perfect for the coast" bedspread and all of the "stuff" that goes with it!

You are probably at this point in the story asking yourself, "Well, why do they care? They already had ordered it!" You're right, but Lynn had recently added a day bed to the room for her daughter, Kara, to sleep on when she came down. She had just told herself that she needed to go back and find the web address from which she had ordered the spread for her bed to get one for Kara's. Now she didn't need to do that. Instead we continued to fill our buggy with the items that were perfect for completing the coastal home's décor.

As you can imagine at this point, it did not take us long to find just the right spread for the youth bed. We started on the aisle before you get to cash registers, and Lynn found a box of wall decorations. We thought it was a bargain for $40 to get black frames to fill our entire wall where the TV rests! I know you want believe this, but it is EXACTLY what we had talked about getting. We had just thought we would have to get more black frames with white mats from various stores to complete the picture in our minds of what the wall should look like. We never guessed we would find it already in one box with a handle for easy transporting!

On the way home, Lynn and I talked about what an amazing day we had had. We both agreed that it goes into our book of Best Days Ever!

Mmm, what do I tell you about next? There is so much happening! I guess I'll tell you what's happening with Alice. You remember her, my Cousin Bill's wife. You know the one I wrote her phone number on the back of her Christmas card envelope. Well, she is the director of an assisted living facility. On the day she got my email about the book, she was at work and wanted to read what I had written. Now, you think that would be easy. On this day, it was not easily accomplished. She sent me at least 3 emails saying she could not open the attachment. So, we tried various things. First, I tried sending it again. Secondly, I sent what I had written as an Open Office document. The third time I tried sending her a new email with the attachments instead of hitting reply.

I did not hear from her until the next day, which was Saturday. Before I share what she wrote, I want you to keep in mind that she has just read the beginnings of this book and is very WELL aware that anything anyone writes as an email to me could very easily be seen by the whole world as a section in this book. This makes me aware that she is cognizant that maybe her email will touch someone's heart in some way. You see I know Alice pretty well, even though we haven't spent that much time together over the twenty something years I've known her.

My Cousin Bill didn't marry her until later in his life. I guess he was waiting for someone as special as Alice. The family all agrees that if Bill divorces Alice then we are keeping Alice and putting Bill out of the family! She has a smile that will warm anyone's heart and makes us laugh with her stories which are usually something funny she has done. I also know that she has been listening to what God has been telling her to do with a lot more faith for far longer than I have.

Here is what she said:

> First of all, let me tell you that I can only open your attachments on my Blackberry. Don't know why, but this morning as I was reading the entire book to this point, it occurred to me that God wanted me to "be still and know that I am God". If I had opened it or printed it, I would probably have been trying to read it somewhere with many interruptions and so on. This Saturday morning it is raining and I've been able to sit with my Blackberry and read and "absorb" what I'm reading.
>
> I know that you know that I've always had a very strong faith, however, we've only talked a little about my upbringing in a Pentecostal church (Assembly of God) and, yes, I mean the rolling in the floor, talking in tongues, divine healing (all healing is divine), full fledged, sold out miracle seeking group. (not snake handling variety) The good news is a strong faith and a belief in miracles. Around my house, miracles were talked about frequently and, if there were problems, miracles were expected and miracles occurred. I'm only saying this to reaffirm my strong belief in prayer, faith, and "speaking into our lives those positive things we expect

as opposed to speaking negativity into our lives and the lives of others.. Our words are powerful. I know that you know all of this, but just in case you were concerned about me thinking you were a little "touched", well, you know that I'm about as "touched" as one can get. I'm most, thankful for that "rooted" faith that I was taught as a child. Even though some of the theology (no makeup (couldn't do without that) or manmade rules were a little "flawed", I still somehow got the basics about "asking and receiving from our Heavenly Father" those things (anything) that we need. Back to the miracles part....I wanted to talk about this back ground now partly because you continue to mention the Holy Spirit. This person in the God Head is not mentioned often. Why is that. Of course, see above, we were taught about the POWER of the Holy Spirit as a child. I don't know if people are afraid to talk about Him. I'm often reminded, as Christians (knowing Christ), that we have access to Again his power any time. We just don't "tap" into Him. Isn't it amazing that all we have to do is call on the Holy Spirit and that power is available yet we very seldom do that?

I'm saying all of this to tell you how excited I am to read every single word of your book. I know that ego (satan) gets in the way and certainly doesn't want to see God's work

prosper, but he (satan) is nothing but a speck
of dirt compared to the Power (Holy Spirit)
we have within us. You refer to Noah and
the great men of the Bible. Yes, I have often
thought about the courage it must have taken
for them to follow God's leading. I used to
think of them as characters when I was a child,
but, as I grew up and realized they were just
ordinary people like you and me, the miracles
God performed through them were even
more inspiring. (Don't you love the old Eddie
Murphy routine about Noah and God?. Really,
I'm not sure I would have built that boat. Read
the story of Gideon again...I would for sure
have been a Gideon. He just kept asking God
to give him another sign...Tried it all kinds of
ways until he finally "got it.. Then when he
"got it" he found out that he had to leave some
of his men behind. I know one thing for sure...
God has a sense of humor. There are so many
downright humorous events in the Bible!

Billy is reading your book and E-Mails......I
know they will be an inspiration to him. I hear
you laughing, but I'm serious, I believe that
Billy has been on a spiritual journey for some
years now....Talk about God working in our
lives. The story of how we all came together is
miraculous in itself. I always say that I know
what God was doing for me. Not sure what He
did to Billy?

O.K......I love you and I am sooooooo looking
forward to seeing you and, of course, Uncle
Jack and Lynn! Yea God!!!. Boo Devil!!!!.
Hope you are ready for a counseling session.
Keep those installments coming. Just can't say
enough about how much I'm enjoying them
and what an inspiration they are. I know that
this book is going to bless so many people.
Thanks for listening to the "Holy Spirit!"

MA

What else should you know about what happened
this week? Oh yea, Lynn and I went on another shopping
trip, and since it involved purchasing a power tool
we drug dad with us, too. Thank goodness the "good
shopping karma" (or God working in mysterious ways)
was still with us! We haven't quite finished our family
coastal home, so Lynn was looking for something to
hold her clothes in her closet. She found just what she
wanted - shelves to go on each side with a bar on which
to hang clothes between the shelves. If any of you have
ever bought this kind of "stuff", then you know it can be
very costly! On that day Lynn got all of that for $50! If
she had bought it on a day where it hadn't been on sale,
then it would have cost her $170!

The other reason we were out shopping was to buy a
printer. I am mostly an electronic gal who doesn't need
to print what I read. I try to save a tree or two whenever
I can, and when I multi-task it is easier to go back and

forth between Windows on my computer and email. I had brought a printer to the coastal house, but had not used it in a very long time.

The reason we needed a printer was for my dad to read what I had written. He has read a little of the beginnings on the computer, but did not care to read anymore on it. I had finished the first part of the book, and my dad had heard my sister and I discussing it. Now, he decided that he wanted to read it. To try and make that happen, the previous day Lynn and I had searched through 2 stores which specialize in office supplies. Neither of them carried the ink for the old printer I'd brought with me to the coastal house. I would have to order it online and wait for it to come. I had just thought that dad wasn't supposed to read it right now. That is the stage in which I find myself now. I am so at peace. God is directing my life. If I listen to him then I will stay at peace, and He will make WONDERFUL things happen!

Earlier that morning right before we got dressed to go shopping, I had read aloud what I had written earlier. Remember I told you Lynn had ADD. After all of my years of teaching, I know that she learns better when she hears something. So, I had read her the latest installment from my computer screen.

After I had finished reading it to Lynn, dad got up from his nap and walked into her bedroom. Lynn and I decided I should read the newest addition for dad, since we didn't seem to be able to print a copy for him any time soon. He enjoyed it so much, that we decided I would just buy another printer if I found an inexpensive one on our shopping outing to buy items to complete the house.

We went to one of those stores that carry items that are over runs or discounted. It was Saturday, so we didn't want to go to a store that was so full of people that you couldn't move. After looking through the entire store and not finding a printer, I thought that God just may not want dad to read it at that time in his life. I figured He just had another better plan in place than the one I thought should happen. Imagine my surprise (or maybe not at this point:-) that I found only one printer in a sealed box right on the shelf in front of the cash register, and it was only $49! It had memory card slots from which to print photos! The ink costs that much! So instead of just buying ink, I ended up with a more updated, better printer than the one I had for less than the price of replacing the ink in my old one. Thank you God for directing my life!

When we got back to the coastal home, I hooked up the printer and printed what I had written so far. Dad, who usually doesn't read for long periods of time, sat and read the first section in its entirety while Lynn and I worked to finish the next stage in decorating the great room.

We used the new printer to print more recent family photos and place in the frames that already hung on the wall from our previous shopping trip. We put words on the wall above the French doors to the side entrance which we use the most. Of course, there is a story with that! You see, Lynn had bought the kit to put the saying on the wall months before along with some angels. At the time I was so immersed in doing whatever I could with this 60 year old body to accomplish that feat (painting, tiling, etc...) that I did not appreciate her purchases. Not only did I not appreciate them, I did not realize that Lynn had been listening to God for far longer than I had, too!

Above our door due to Lynn's purchases are now the words, "FAMILY… a journey to forever." There are angels around the words. Each one has only one word on it. The words found on them are – Hope, Love, Blessings, Peace, and Joy. Do you think it is a coincidence that the word "journey" is part of the subtitle of this book? I know that Peace and Joy are 2 of the words that are often in my lessons from *A Course in Miracles*. I also know that I am receiving countless Blessings from all of the Love I am feeling and know that my family and friends along with me are feeling Hope for a brighter future. **God are you talking to me? I am experiencing boundless blessings because I am listening to you!**

There are some things that God has directed me to do this week which have yet to come to fruition. In other words, I have sent out messages to other people about my spiritual journey and have not received any words back from any of them except Alice. At this point in my peaceful, joyful journey I realize that it is just not in God's plan to happen right now. But, the afternoon of the 5th day of this week is upon me and the ego is trying desperately to start putting me in a panic about what I am going to write about tomorrow in order for me to rest on the 7th day!

You see, I do not know how to tell you about how the actual "writing" takes place. You've been on this journey with me, yet I have not given you many details. At this point in the story, if I were the reader, my inquisitive mind would want to know more in order to have confirmation that this crazy story is for real!

Here is what I do know. Unlike J. K. Rowling's Harry Potter series (which I couldn't wait to read each installment and am very sad that there will be no more) which was basically mapped out ahead of time or Helen Schucman's *A Course in Miracles* which she wrote with an "inner dictation", I am not sure what I am going to write each day or what that message is supposed to be.

At the beginning the writing was almost frantic. All I felt like I was doing was trying to write down words that will spark some recognition about what I think God wants me to talk about and sometimes string them into sentences and then into paragraphs. After the first few days a form in which I mix the conversations I am having with God calling myself the character "self" and relating what is happening in my life underneath the conversations just sort of happened. I wanted to have as much humor in it as possible, because now that I think about it being able to make people laugh has always been one of the things I have wished I could do! Being an author of inspirational books was NEVER on my list of things I wanted to do!

Now I wake up almost every morning somewhere between 4 and 4:30. First I say my "Rules for Decisions" from *A Course in Miracles*, and then I stay very still in my bed and try to hear God's voice. Since I was raised as a Presbyterian, It is a small quiet voice. I think you hear God's voice in the way you need to hear it. I told you about how frightened as a child I would get when Reverend Burrell would deliver God's message in a loud, booming voice, so I don't think God will ever talk to me that way and don't want Him to! Yet, if you want to hear Him that way, then I believe you will. I also believe you hear Him in music, see Him in beautiful works of art or nature, or hear and see Him on the big movie screen or on the smaller (sometimes not smaller now) TV sets in your home. In other words, He is all around us talking to us. All we have to do is recognize Him.

While I am lying in bed trying to hear God's voice, what I'm supposed to write for the day just comes to me. Somewhere around 5 I reach over and grab my computer. I awaken it from sleeping and spend the next part of my day reading and meditating on whatever the next Lesson from *A Course in Miracles* is. After that I switch over from my lesson to this document that will become this book and begin typing for usually 2 to 3 hours. Now when you think about it, 2 to 3 hours a day averages out to 2.5 "ish". When you take 10% of the 24 hours of a day, my giving God his 10% of time is about that (can you tell I taught math). Is that a coincidence? You know what I think without me even saying it!

Back to the afternoon of the fifth day of the week and I don't have anything to write about. I know you know what is coming next! I get a return email from my friend Elissa. Elissa has been my friend the longest (in this body form at least) and was the other teen that had her ears pierced by Cousin Maggie with the promise of getting a pair of her earrings in the future. When you talk about the amount of time that we have been together in this life, it will be very difficult for many people to beat it. How can that be, you are probably asking yourself? Well, Elissa's mother was 3 months pregnant with her and in the delivery room when my mother delivered me! Let me see any of you can beat that!

Now, let me see if I can explain our relationship. We always called ourselves cousins and down here in the south that can mean many things. It could mean your family has known a family for generations or it could mean you are connected by blood. Elissa's and my relationship is somewhere in between. Remember Maggie who carried Lynn around on her hip for the first 3 months of her life and I told you that she was my mother's cousin, well she was Elissa's father's (the one that called Lynn, Imp) cousin, too. In other words, my great uncle (the other one who called Lynn, Imp) married Elissa's great aunt and had Maggie. So, anytime Uncle Albert or Aunt Lila had a family gathering that would include Elissa's family and my family, but there would be no sense in asking me to see if I were a match if Elissa needed a kidney transplant, though I would gladly do it.

Our parents were good friends. Why wouldn't they be? You see dad and Francis were best friends growing up. Their parents at one time lived a few doors down from one another. Francis introduced dad to his cousin by marriage, Myra. They got married and had me and my siblings.

Elissa and I shared many of life's adventures. When she lived up here (one traumatic time in our lives her parents moved them all to Florida), we went to Sunday School and children's choir together, though often we were not in the same class together. The 6 months that separates our ages put me in a grade ahead of her, as my birthday in is December and when I went to school you could start at 5. We also at times were in the same school building, but not the same classes.

Some of my happiest times as a child are centered on our joint family vacations! Most every summer both families would pool resources and would go camping on a lake where we could water ski. We children would stay in a tent and play cards, Monopoly, and Clue until we were too tired from the day's water activities to keep our eyes opened any longer. Even then, Elissa and I would whisper way into the night about whatever young people talked and wondered about. Of course, with Elissa's memory (I often call her my memory to her face, since I erased so much of my childhood from my brain) she could probably relate word for word most of those conversations we had.

So, you can see how important it was for me that Elissa would enjoy the book. I knew she would support me, because she had always supported anything I ever did (even my first marriage which she knew would be a disaster). But, in my mind Elissa would be the writer first. Her father and his family had always written humorous pieces, and Elissa and her siblings had inherited the skill. Aunt Lila was the one who was always giving us children inspirational books, so in my mind Elissa should be writing this – NOT me!

I was not concerned that it had been days since I sent her the email and attachment. At this point "the peace that passeth all understanding" is with me most of the time. I knew it was part of God's plan for me to receive her phone call or get her email when He thought the time was right. So, by now you can see that right before the panic set in (you know the ego was trying for me to believe that like it did with Lynn that Elissa was not going to like it and not know what to say to me) on the 5th afternoon, Elissa's email came. Again, all of my friends have been forewarned once they have read the book and know that their emails are fair game for this book, so here's Elissa's.

> Hello, You've been on my mind and I
> wondered if I was going to have to call out
> the South Georgia Mafia to find you. Had an
> argument with myself and thought you had
> decided that I could just fall into ole Lake
> Hartwell, cause you were having so much fun
> at your new home....you do know that you are
> in the very area (almost the exact spot) that
> the Presbyterian Church was established in

Georgia ....I took Mother Laurie to the 250th celebration in Darien while I lived down that way.

What a special journey. I've read all of your e-mails and details you've sent so far (-- what did Mrs. Watkins know. You write beautifully, and with such humor!!!. No need for you to ask, You know that you have my absolute support.....please you'll give me a call if you need for me to see something ASAP as I don't see my e-mails but about once a week!!!

My love and God's Blessings....your Best Friend Forever!

Elissa

I am so blessed to have family and friends which so heartedly support me! I do not ever read one of these emails without tears of joy leaking onto my face. If you ask any of these people, they will say, "Yes, that's Tana. She cries at the drop of a hat."

I sent an email back to her to let her know how much I appreciate her and her kind words, and a few minutes later I received another one from her. This is unusual in this journey, but getting used to unusual things happening in my life is becoming "usual"! She replied in the next email with:

I feel compelled to ask you to read the book of First Peter.....It's only 5 chapters and you can read one a day.....just doing what I'm lead to do....

Elissa's reference to the Bible was the second time I had been given that message today. I am at the stage in this journey where I can question whether what I am thinking is me or God after one time, but the second time is a completely different story! I reached over beside my bed and pulled out my Bible and read the chapters. I will read them again today to make sure I got the entire message.

Now if you read these chapters from Peter, you will see like I did that there is confirmation that what I am doing and the journey on which I am going is not as strange as it first seemed. **Thank you God, for sending me more signs through my family and friends that I am hearing Your voice! Thank you God for friends and family who are listening to You and relaying to me what You said to me to make sure I get it!**

6
Week Three

God, how do any of Your children learn to hear Your voice?

Self: Good morning, Father! Here I am waiting to hear what you want me to say next in this book You've told me to write. What is it you want me to write today?

Self: You want me to say, "God loves you!" But, doesn't everybody know that? I've always known it!

Self: I forget that some people in their own projection booths thinking that they are separated from You are writing their life scripts with horrible things going on in them. I know that there are awful things happening in the world, too. I also know that You have blessed me, my family, and my friends with many wonderful things. But God, is telling them You love them going to be enough?

Self: Okay God, they need to hear Your voice to feel more of Your love, and anybody can open that channel of communication with You in order to more readily experience more of Your love and blessings. I mean, I know a little about how to do that. First of all, I know that Your son, Jesus, went off by Himself into the wilderness to talk to You, I read in Gary Renard's book *The Disappearance of the Universe* that he, like me, practiced the lessons in *A Course in Miracles* to more readily hear You, and at the end of Depok Chokra's book *Jesus: A Story of Enlightenment* there are details for going on a path to come closer to You. Which one am I supposed to tell people to use? What is it You want me to say to help people in order for them to more easily hear Your voice?

Self: Oh, okay. There are different ways of doing this. And, You're saying that someone could follow the prescribed one in *A Course in Miracles* like Gary and I did. What's another one?

Self: Is it that simple?

Self: All anyone has to do is find 5 minutes or so in the morning when one wakes up and another 5 at night before they go to bed. But God, don't many people already do that when they pray to you at those times?

Self: Got it! They talk to you, but You can't get a word in edgewise because they do not quiet all of their thoughts about all of the things they have to do, or their minds are focused on the problems they were just praying about. So, how do they get still and quiet their minds, so they can hear You?

Self: Okay, they can't focus on pushing the thoughts out of their minds, because then their thoughts are busy doing exactly what they are trying to prevent from happening. So, how do they quiet their minds so they can hear You?

Self: Oh, since You are Love, they are to surround those thoughts that the ego keeps trying to push in their minds with love and those thoughts will just gradually disappear. If they do that, will they hear You right away? I mean I heard You, yet I didn't know I was hearing you.

Self: You're right God; from the very beginning of this journey my higher self (the one that is on a first name basis with the Holy Spirit) was doing a LOT of talking, now that I think about it! I mean how else did all of those miraculous things start happening with me and my family! But, I didn't start really recognizing that some of my thoughts were You talking to me in a still, quiet voice until you told me to write this book a couple of weeks ago, and even then I wasn't sure it was You.

Self: And, you also want me to tell them not to get discouraged if they don't hear You right away. Believe me I know that one! I had tried to listen to You for almost a 100 days before I really heard You and recognized it was Your voice. I remember waiting for some big sign while I was listening to you to know I was doing the right thing! I was waiting for some big white light or my spirit to take flight and visit whomever I wanted to go see without paying for a plane ticket. But, none of those things happened! But, eventually I started hearing You, and I do feel very peaceful when I am listening for Your voice. Do I need to worry about telling them anything else?

Self: I got it. I'm to stop worrying about it, because when they start listening You can take it from there! Whew, I'm always glad when You step in, and I know everything is going to be just fine! Catch You later!

Events of Week 3

"Okay God, it's the day I'm supposed to write about what is happening this week, and I haven't experienced any miracles to confirm to the reader Your active presence in my life. Most of my friends even though they are sending me supportive emails are probably afraid to say much more than that in order to stay out of the book! I didn't go on any big shopping trips to experience "good shopping karma" (thank goodness as I won't have to spend any money as my budget for this month's extras is depleted). The only way I know You're still here and I'm doing what you want me to do is You keep sending me signs that You are pleased with my progress. Yesterday when you had Josh Groban's voice singing *You Raise Me Up* play on my Zune, I really listened to the words. I know it was You telling me I could do this- write a book inspired by You- thing! And, physically the vibrations throughout my body are at such a low hum that I seldom realize that they are present now (Oh God, I appreciate your sending me the Beach Boy's voices singing "I'm picking up good vibrations; they're bringing me excitations" to go with those vibrations), so I'm beginning to panic a little bit while waiting for your inspiration to come," I thought when I pulled out my computer to begin to write this morning. Then I thought about what I had just written. "Good shopping karma" and experiencing physical vibrations, oh I'm supposed to write about my conversations with the daughter of my heart, Danette!

Let me give you a little more background on Danette. She's the one that keeps me youthful! When we go to the movies, I know I can count on her to want to see the ones that young or young at heart would want to experience. I go with her to be taken away to the world of fantasy. Jeanie on the other hand wants to see character development when we go to the movies. When I go with Danette we go see one of the Harry Potter movies or something like *The Lion, the Witch, and the Wardrobe*. I can always count on her to say things like, "*Wicked* is playing at the Fox! Let's get tickets and go!" And, she will make the arrangements and plan to make this happen! She introduces me to new musical artists she thinks I may enjoy and makes sure that we get to hear some of them in concert.

Okay, I've told you about how she keeps me young using the arts, but she also dresses me. I mean not physically put my clothes on, but Danette takes me shopping with her. First of all, to keep mom 2's (that's what she calls me)clothes in style and secondly to let her "good shopping karma" be experienced by me! You see,

Danette was the first one, as far as I know, to coin that term for what she has. And, she has it! Whenever I go shopping with Danette, everything is ridiculously low priced! No wonder she has such a hard time staying on a budget with always finding such bargains!

The other way she keeps me in style is by giving me her clothes. You see, we're always on a diet, and she always does better than me (I say it's because she's got the younger than me thing going). Once she's lost a pants size, then she gives them to me. Of course, right now I can't stand those pants riding so low on my hips, but my daughter of my heart gives them to me and I wear them!

Well, now that you sort of understand the role she plays in my life, I can tell you about how she wrote herself into this book.

I didn't get any response to my emails and beginnings of book attachments for the first couple of weeks. Like I've told you before, I'm really at peace with letting God's plan unfold on His timeline, not mine. I know his plan for my soul's best growth is ALWAYS much better than mine. I know Danette's life is busy with work and family. I also figured that Danette's part in this journey was going to be significant, and she would need her own section! It seems like she does.

Here's how she writes herself in. I get a phone call from her from school. Since her students are so important to her, she does not call me during school hours. This means something is the matter. Because she has anxiety attacks and gets anxious about taking her anxiety medicine (which makes no sense to me, but seems to be the case with a lot of people with anxiety issues), she usually calls me to say to her, "Just take the d_ _ _ medicine!" I am not usually forceful with anything (again just ask any of these friends), so my using these words and this tone conveys to her its important and do it now! She always laughs and takes the medicine. Since I'm not at school this year to tell her that, she has given that job to Patti who is across the hall from her. So when she calls, I do not think that is what she is calling me for; but her voice is in its panic mode. She said, "I've not been able to sleep the past couple of nights, my body is shaking all over most of the time, and I don't know what's the matter with me. Patti (who has read the entire book so far and knows I am experiencing these type of vibrations) said I should call you."

Now when I hear her say the body is shaking all over part of her symptoms, I just start giggling inside. Not laughing at her panic (never – as it is NOT a laughing matter), but laughing with God who has sent Danette and I a sign that whatever He has planned for us we will be going through it together. I have to wait for her to take a breath and tell her it is going to be all right; that I have been experiencing the same thing which is a sign from God. Danette and I have been through some mystical things together, and I know that is all I have to say. She relayed to me that just that morning she had been talking with another one of our friends about not being happy and thinking she wanted to write a book (is that a coincidence- I DON'T think so!). I then went into as much detail about what has been happening with

me as I can in a short amount of time. I didn't want to keep her from her students, but I knew I had to give her enough assurance that she was going to be fine. I also knew she would call me on her drive home in order for us to have a few more minutes to talk before she gets home to her 3 children under the age of 9. When she called back, I told her about sending an email to those going on this journey with me and suggesting that some of them might want to think about writing a book. I said to her again, "You said this morning that you were thinking about writing a book, you have an email waiting in your inbox which you haven't read that suggests you write a book, you have the vibrations in your body I've had since I started writing this book, so don't you think you need to listen to all of these signs?" She replied, "Yes, and my mother (who also shares with her daughter mystical experiences) suggested I write a book just the other day."
Is God talking to you, Danette?

Thank goodness Danette listened. She took the weekend to read some of my book and have family time. Monday she called me on her way home from school. She was so excited! Her voice resonated with her happiness through the phone's speaker. She told me she had decided to write a book to help teens using a format similar to mine. In fact, she had almost finished the first chapter! She said she was still having trouble sleeping (I know that feeling), but now it was because she was either writing her book or getting her inspiration to write it! The joy that one feels when the soul chooses to fulfill the possibility that is most aligned with what God created that soul to do is beyond explaining!

As I later contemplate what has happened and what it means, God hits me over the head with the realization that this book is a way to get to my real heart's desire. You know by now that I NEVER wanted to be an author. I HATE speaking in public, and I know that anyone who writes a book has to go on tour and speak to promote it! Let's not think about that now! It makes my heart race just to write it down! I mean the only way I got through the few times I've had to speak in public I had to have anxiety drugs myself! Don't think about it, Tana. Don't think about it. Don't think about it. Instead let the love surround it and make it disappear as a thought in my brain (Please, God!).

Let's get back to my real heart's desire. While I've been on this journey, I've come to the realization that when 2 or more people have the same desire that it is VERY powerful when you throw Jesus and the Holy Spirit into the mix! (Side note- Do you know what song started playing as I type this? Yep- Josh Groban's *You Raise Me Up* to more than I can be!) From the time when Danette and I first became friends, do you know what we used to talk about the most when we had time together? Most of our conversations were about how to help our alternative school help more kids. We were always asking ourselves what we could do differently to make a difference in those children's lives. Now, God is telling me that this book is just one step in my soul's journey to obtaining my heart's greatest desire – helping kids! I'll just have to wait and see how God makes that happen. His plan is SO much bigger, grander, and better than the one I had in place!

God, I am listening to you and learning to have the patience for your plan to unfold on Your Timeline!

Oh, I almost forgot to tell you about the printer! You remember my old printer for which I couldn't find ink. Remember I thought dad wasn't supposed to read my book right then, because I couldn't find ink and I bought another better one that prints photos. Here I was thinking God was telling me I needed a better printer, but there He goes again having a better plan for my printer than any I could imagine. Here's how this part of my life's spiritual story unfolded.

This past weekend Alice (the one who couldn't read my book except on her Blackberry even after many forms of it had been sent to her email) and Cousin Bill visited. Cousin Bill likes visiting the historic places in the area and always plans for us to see a little bit of history each time he comes. So, Saturday we were off to see Fort Morris and Fort McAllister. Today was supposed to be one of those days where my lesson from *A Course in Miracles* was supposed to be thought about every half hour. I was wondering how I was going to make that happen and decided to send the lesson as an email to my Blackberry so I would have it. I copied and pasted the words I was supposed to repeat on the half hour into an email and sent it to my phone. I had my computer opened, so I checked my email. There was an email from Carol about Jaye having an interview for a job he really wanted and to say prayers for him. I looked at the time and realized the email had come yesterday. Why hadn't I gotten it on my phone from yesterday yet? I looked at my phone and had one of those automatic messages that said I needed to put my password in again. Now, this had never happened before (along with all of these other things that have never happened to me before). I followed both sets of instructions and after numerous tries; I decided that God was telling me not to worry about the lesson today. Today was for spending time with my earthly family, and I had another one of those days that will go into my best days list (minus the fool with phone time)!

Once, we got back home I tried to figure out how to get my personal email (I was still getting my online university email) to continue coming to my phone. Alice kept telling me that when it had happened to her, that she had to call and have them reset it. Being the stubborn person that I am and determined to figure it out on my own, I continued to try and make it work. Finally after deleting it and restoring the personal email, I could get my email on my phone! Do I think it was coincidence; no I do not!

Sunday morning came and Alice asked me if I was going to the church in Savannah that I thought God had directed me to go to. I told her that I had learned that God's plan for me changes, and I was not to go. You see I had decided I was going to go, because God had directed me to do so. Then Alice had said she would go with me and my sister had said she would go, too. My sister got sick and could not come down. Alice and Bill had decided to leave earlier that day to be home in time to watch the Super Bowl, so she couldn't go either. When

I think God tells me something, I realize it could be the ego if I hear it only once, but the second time assures me it is Him. My sister was one person who had backed out and Alice was the second one, so I concluded that He didn't need me to go right now. When you hear the rest of the story, then you will know why.

As Alice and I were talking and Bill was loading the car with their things, I reminded Alice that I thought she should compile her columns into an inspirational book. You see, Alice writes a monthly column in her local newspaper titled *Let's Talk* (do I think it is a coincidence that Alice's column and my book both have the word "talk" in it – you know what I think). Her articles are inspirational and humorous. Alice told me she felt like she was supposed to write a compiled book of her articles, but had been too busy to do it yet. I told her I felt like she should get it together this year. She listens to God all the time and believes I am passing on His message to her (yes – I am getting pretty accustomed to doing what He tells me to do even if it is saying to someone to write a book). She started thinking about what she needed to get done to make the book happen. She said she had all of the newspaper clippings in files at home; even though she had lost some of the electronic versions during computer crashes. Since she was thinking about compiling a daily inspirational book, she wanted the clippings to be in order by their dates. She would need to scan the articles into an electronic format in her computer, but she didn't have a scanner at home. If she did, then Bill who is so good with details could work on it for her from home. But wait, I have a scanner on the printer for which I couldn't find the ink under the bed in front of which we are standing! I tell her about it, as I pull it out from under the bed. She says that she can order the ink without a problem, because they have Dell computers at work. Oh, and she had just told me that her printer tore up recently! Here I thought the printer was about dad reading this book, but all along it was God's plan that it helps Alice get her book compiled! **God, thank you for having a much better plan than mine, and one that enables each of us to be a blessing through You to one or all of Your children!**

7
Week Four

God, how do any of Your children learn to have faith when they are beginning to hear Your voice and wait on You to manifest Your blessings?

Self: God, I couldn't wait until our conversation today to thank you for answering my prayers!

Self: You know the one I have been praying for so long now. The one where I can truly not worry about money and believe that you will take care of my needs just like you do with the lilies of the field and birds in the air.

Self: You remember God I have always had a strong faith that You would take care of me. I may have had to eat p & j sandwiches, but I've always gotten by-by Your grace (even though I experienced it some of the time through my parent's generosity).

Self: Well God, you know how empathetic I am, so I couldn't stop worrying about money when my son has had such problems with it! I mean he hasn't been able to make his house payments in months after doing a job and losing thousands of dollars. I mean most of that money that was owed to him was to pay for the materials that were used to do the job, so there sure wasn't any money to pay himself a salary to pay his bills! You know I was more than glad to help out, but a teacher's salary sure doesn't pay enough to pay his vendors!

Self: Yes, I know You and Waylon have been having some long conversations lately. Of course, we've been having some long ones lately, too! Last Sunday, he talked to me for almost 3 hours and watched 10 different church services on TV, and there is no telling how much he talked to You! You know why, too! Again, 2 weeks had gone by without his getting his contracted draw from a job from a public school renovation. He turned in his bill when the job was done last month and has waited more than another month to get the money he was promised. Now it is 2 more weeks past that and he still hasn't received the money. Waylon thought that job would be a safe one. You know he has so much love in his heart that he doesn't care about the money for himself except to provide for Dana and Jadelyn. He just can't stand not being able to pay the few people he is able to try and keep giving work to. I mean he has borrowed money from the family to pay their salaries and keep going a couple more weeks, but it was evident that he was at his lowest point Sunday and Monday.

Self: I know, You gave him a sign the next night. He told me he had a dream and that he usually doesn't remember them. The next morning he remembered that a woman in the dream had told him to read John 10:10. He said that he was frightened for a moment that it would be one of those obscure verses, but it wasn't. I mean how could he not get Your message when he read: "The thief comes only to steal and kill and destroy; I come that they may have life, and have it abundantly." I know that he does feel as if the contractors who haven't had the money to pay him have stolen his money and he does so want to believe in Your abundant blessings like the last part of the verse affirms he should. Waylon does feel blessed in the love of his family and friends, but it has been so hard for him to believe that he is Your child and deserves so much more of your blessings. Thank you, God for giving him that sign! It helped him hang on for the rest of the week and deal with the disappointment of not getting the money when Friday came again and the contractor was unable to pay him.

Self: I am SO grateful for the next sign You sent him though! Did you hear the excitement and wonder in his voice when he told me? I wish I could have seen his face like You did when he opened my mailbox while checking my mail and found an envelope addressed to him. He told me he thought it was someone else that he owed money to which was suing him. He said at this point he could just add it to the pile that continues to grow. I mean what else can he do? He works 6 or 7 days a week and puts in 10 or 12 hours a day, yet it seems for no money. Without You he would have given up a long time ago!

Oh yeah, back to the story. He opened up the envelope and there was a check for almost $800 from his closing on his house years ago! I mean it is like the one dad got unexpectedly, but his closing was only a month ago. You have done really well, God, with making unexpected money appear to help my dad and Waylon REALLY believe that you will provide! Oh, and I forgot that Jaye got that life insurance dividend check that mom paid on for all those years that he didn't know about either! So all those important men in my life are REALLY **getting Your message that You will provide and have faith that abundant blessings are in our future!**

Self: Yes, I know that $800 is enough for him to put gas in his car and food on his table and hold out a few days longer. I think he really believes this contractor is telling him the truth, and he will have the money he is owed this week. I sure hope so! But, You also sent him more work when he hadn't even put bids out to get any, so that is helping him feel like he can make it!

Self: Oh God speaking of dreams, I wanted to tell you how much I enjoyed the dream you sent me. Like Waylon, You know I don't usually remember mine either, but this morning I woke up and felt like I had been on a vacation! I remember swimming in a pool and going on a "sort of" date (really a date- I haven't been on one of those in YEARS) with some Irish "Hugh Laurie" type (looks – not the *House* character – UGH) of guy. We ate ice cream! I had fun! Are you trying to tell me something or having me go on a dream date in preparation for the real thing?

Self: Yes, I know by now that I am to be at peace, have patience, and You will answer that question when You are good and ready and when it is best for my soul's growth and development! It's been great talking with You, and I know we'll talk again really soon.

Events of Week Four

How do I tell you about the blessings this week have brought? I have been providing evidence about things that are happening in my life each day and now each week that confirm God's blessings, but now that evidence is not so readily available to the physical eyes I'm not sure about what to say. Since the bodies' eyes cannot prove it to you, then you are just going to have faith in what I tell you is the truth.

Remember I told you about the awful feeling that came over me when my Grandmother died; well that is the only time I have had any type of what may be some sort of psychic experience that involved knowing something ahead of when this body got the message in the usual way – like a telephone call or face-to-face conversation. But, since I have been studying *A Course in Miracles,* that is no longer true.

Like I felt when I didn't want to tell my family and friends that I was writing a book which God had told me to write and when God wanted me to tell my friends to do certain things, that is how I feel now when God has told me it is time to tell you about the things He has told me are going to happen and which you would label as my precognition experiences.

I have told you about driving by my dad's house and seeing a car and realizing that he would soon have the house sold. Now, that could have been just my seeing the realtor's car and making a lucky guess. I agree, as I had my doubts in the beginning when I got these feelings that God was telling me certain things were going to happen. Once, yes would have been just a lucky guess, but it happening over and over again is NOT a coincidence!

Today it is very difficult for me to remember the first time. I think it must have been when my sister Lynn heard from Gia, the daughter she gave up at birth, when she contacted her by email. When they had first made contact 10 years ago, Lynn was very disappointed she was not able to meet her. She had celebrated her birthday unbeknownst to Gia every year with Lynn's wish that she was somewhere healthy, happy, and much loved. When Gia was not ready to pursue their relationship after the initial contact, Lynn tried to be content with the thoughts that she knew she was alive and seemed to be loved and happy.

For the past 10 years, Lynn has tried to be content with the gift of knowing Gia was okay. She knew many mothers that give their children up for adoption never have any contact with them. Lynn was elated when she and Gia made contact again. She hoped this time she would get to actually be able to see her, but was afraid to hope so much that she could be disappointed again.

When Lynn told me she and Gia had started emailing each other once again, I told her that they would meet this time. I didn't tell Lynn that it was a message through me from God. I hadn't started talking with anyone at that point about my very intimate experiences I was having with Him. It was too personal at the time, I wasn't sure anyone would believe me, and I wasn't really sure it was God talking to me.

Gia set a date for their meeting, and Lynn was so excited about it! When Gia had to cancel, Lynn was so disappointed. I gave her all the reasons I could to try and reassure her that it would happen this time. I said things like, "She has 2 children, a husband, and a full time job. Things like this happen." I was doing everything I could to convince her it was going to happen without telling her how I knew it would.

Lynn waited, and Gia set another date for their meeting. It DID happen that time! You can only imagine the joy Lynn has received with that occurrence! The only thing that would make her life more joyful now is meeting Maya and Jake, her grandchildren. I have told her that would come, too. Jake's birthday party is coming very soon, and Lynn has been invited to it! **God's blessings continue to come to those who honor Him and stay in faith!**

The other event I knew was going to happen this year is the healing of Lynn's back. I told you already that she has worn opiate patches to control the excruciating pain she has had in her back for years now. Lynn has been unable to truly enjoy much of life's adventures because of the debilitating pain. It is not completely well yet, but the pain is much more manageable today and allows her to begin to take part in life's journey more fully than she has in a long time.

The next event I predicted would happen, I have laid the groundwork to give you a little evidence of it ahead of time. Remember earlier in the book that I said I was saving a secret to be told to you later; well here is one of them. Of course, you could say I could put anything in here and not really have known it. You're right. I could say anything right now. You have to choose at this point whether you believe God gives his gifts of love today to His children. You have to choose whether you think this sounds like your God. Like *A Course in Miracles* says, every one of God's children will learn this, but they all get to choose when they want to receive His word.

Remember when Lynn and I went out to eat lunch on one of our shopping trips and we talked about my mother's ring that I wore and how she thought I ought to separate it and make the ruby bands earrings. Well, what I didn't tell you was that I was planning on asking Jaye if he wanted the original wedding band portion of the ring to give to Carol before Lynn even knew I was thinking about doing that. And Jaye had not said anything about asking Carol to marry him at that time. Again, you can say that it was my intuition after seeing how happy Carol and Jaye are together, but I know what I believe. Today I am happy to be able to tell you that the original wedding band looks beautiful on Carol's hand as an engagement ring! I had to go back and add this after Jaye asked Carol to marry him, because there was no way I was going to give away the surprise for Carol as she's been reading each of these installments!

So now you know another one of my little secrets, God is telling me His Love is coming and He is giving me specifics! **Thank you God for your abundant, eternal Love for all of Your children!**

8
Week Five

God, how do all of Your children learn to experience only Your Love?

Self: God, thank you for my Valentine's Day gift!

Self: I thought it was so cool that the night before you had Waylon send me a text to re-read First Corinthians 13. I just LOVE that last part you wrote. "Now we see but a poor reflection as in a mirror; then we shall see face to face. Now I know in part; then I shall know fully, even as I am fully known. And now these three remain: faith, hope and love. But the greatest of these is love." So, I go to bed with those words in my head and wake up on Valentine's Day. I open up *A Course in Miracles* to study my lesson and spend quality time with You. To my surprise (not really any more:-) the lesson is titled

"There is no love but God's." I thought that lesson was PERFECT for the day!

Self: Oh, that's what You want me to tell everyone about today! You are so funny! You make me giggle all the time with the way you send me messages and the content of them! You keep reminding me that this journey should be JOYFUL!

Self: Right, I'm getting off topic. So, what do you want me to start with?

Self: Okay, you want me to tell them again that this world is not the real word. But Father, that concept is so difficult to understand! I mean you had to send Jesus to experience it, because You couldn't. I mean if we are all One with You all of the time, then if You thought You were separate from us to experience this, then You wouldn't be one with us!

Self: Oh, that's the point. You have never left us, because You are Love and it is One. What do You mean by Love is One?

Self: Got it! Like my lesson from *A Course in Miracles* said, "Love has no separate parts and no degrees; no kinds nor levels, no divergencies and no distinctions. It is like itself, unchanged throughout. It never alters with a person or a circumstance. It is the heart of God, and also of His Son."

Self: So, what You're saying is that the love we think we experience in this world can't be Your True Love; because here we withhold our love for some people, give it to some people, think that there is "puppy love", and think that there are special people who deserve all of our love. But, Your love is the only true meaning of love. Your Love is the same for everyone, because every one is loved the same for all eternity and that love never changes.

Self: Let me see if I have this right. If we want to experience more of the real world or Heaven on earth until it's time for us to be in Heaven where TRUE LOVE resides and is effortless but just is, then we must strive to love everyone all of the time.

Self: But Father, you have no idea how difficult that is here! I mean when someone seems to hurt you in any way, then you just want to retaliate.

Self: That's right. I forget that if I am separate from them, then there is no way that I can know what script of life we would have written together, if I had included that person's TRUE thoughts and love in on the script. I mean that person is my brother or sister! It doesn't matter what I see on the outside; each person is one of Your children and deserves nothing but LOVE! If I want to experience more of what it's like to have Heaven on earth, then I need to remember that all of the time! If I'm to live like You want me to live and experience all of Your blessings, then I am not supposed to ever say anything unkind. Instead I'm to say nothing when anyone appears to wrong me, and I'm to bless them with Your love with my thoughts.

Self: Oh Father when I bless them with Your Love, I am joined with You in YOUR TRUE LOVE and we are joined in thoughts which is more like it is in the real world. Okay, I think I got it! That must be the reason I'm hearing that song in my head now singing, "I'm in Heaven. I'm in Heaven."

Self: Thank you Father for that song. I sort of feel like I'm floating on air and dancing with Fred Astaire when I hear it!

Self: So, You think that's enough for right now?

Self: Okay, I'll talk to you later.

Events of Week Five

To tell you about this stage of my journey, I have to go back to "Day 0". You know, the day that preceded the night when I got the message to write this book. At this point in my life's spiritual awakening story, I had completed reading *A Course in Miracles* text for the third time. I was about a fourth of the way through the course's lessons. That is the farthest I have ever gotten with the lessons in mind training. In the previous two attempts, I had tried to do as Jesus had instructed and complete them, but never had. Previously when I had attempted to get through the lessons, I would feel very guilty when I would read the instructions in a day's Lesson and ask myself, "How am I going to spend 15 minutes twice a day, when I have to be a mother, teacher, friend, and whatever else one has to do in any one day and still find time to dedicate that much time to doing this?" In other words, the ego would find numerous excuses for me not to complete them. Today I realize that that time in my life was the beginning of the foundation for *A Course in Miracles* basic principles, but not the time to really begin the mind training which is necessary for this leg of my spiritual journey. The Bible says that for every season, there is a time. *A Course in Miracles* states that it is a required course, and only the time necessary to take it is a choice.

In the leg of my journey to spiritual awakening of which I am writing, I had seen flashes of light during the times I had closed my eyes to practice the Lessons. I was not frightened by this, because *A Course in Miracles* says that you might experience some flashes of light. But, some of the other things that occurred were very frightening to me. There was the night I couldn't sleep after seeing the broadcast on my computer in which the Master Teacher had said, "You are coming home." I did not know whether my body was just going to disappear or whether the body was going to experience what we humans conceive of as "die". All I could think about was who was going to finish my online class (as final grades were due that week) and who was going to pay my mortgage on my house. What would my family and friends who depended on me do? I lay there most of the night with my body vibrating at such a high level, that I thought it was just going to dissipate into the universe. Today, I know the ego was making a desperate attempt to hold on to itself. It was that night that I asked for the love to replace the fear and for the knowledge to be given to me to never be afraid of what was happening to me during this spiritual journey. The next morning

I practiced A *Course In Miracles Rules for Decisions*, read my lesson for the day, meditated the required 5 minutes for that hour, and then went to hear my broadcast from the Master Teacher. When I went to the tab for the broadcast, I could not remember whether I was just supposed to hit the button and make it play or if I had not gone to the next lesson. For me this was unusual, because I always knew what was next. When I began to watch it, I realized it was a repeat of the one I had seen yesterday where the Master Teacher had told me I was coming home. Normally, I would have gone on to the next video, but that day I thought that I was supposed to watch it again. I was learning to listen to God. While I was watching it again, I figured if I watched it again and nothing physically happened to me, then it would reassure me and help replace the fear with love. I watched the next video on *Mastertv* and then went about my day finishing grades for my online class.

In the move from my dad's house into the coastal house, I had just put things somewhere to get them out of the way. When I went to take a bath that day, I saw my mother's copy of Shirley McClain's *Going Within* in the basket in the bathroom. I opened up and began reading. In it I found more reassurance that this body was physically safe. I began to start realizing that everyone's journey is different, because it must be a personal exploration. I also began to understand that the basic principles are the same – Love and One God.

I am a big AI (American Idol for those who are not ardent fans) fan, and it was the beginning of a new season. You know the part where they are showing the auditions. Now, I do not want to miss the opportunity to choose who I think may be the next AI, but tonight was different. I had the TV on, but was looking for a study group for *A Course In Miracles*. I had searched online for one before and got to the part where you put in your email and other identifying info and just did not want to do it. Then, I looked at churches in the area. I knew I liked the message that female pastors give, as it matched my beliefs more. I knew that the ministers at the Presbyterian and Methodist churches in the closest town were not females. I had attended a Unity church with a friend of my mother's earlier in my life, when I had read *A Course in Miracles* text the first time. I read more about the Unity church online in a search and found one close by me. There was a female minister which was another plus. I explored their website. I listened to a podcast. Yet still I was not sure it was the church for me, as I was not sure I needed a church and would have to travel about an hour to attend services.

Next in my search for reassurance of love and not fear, I began to search for terms that Master Teacher had been using such as anthropically and home illumanati. I figured if these terms were there, then that was more evidence that there was nothing to fear. While searching I came across Gary Renard and his website. I was able to read some excerpts from his books. I watched his hour podcast on PlanetChange.TV. In all of this, I felt as if here was God talking to me again to reinforce the concept that we are all on an individual spiritual awakening journey that have different paths, but many of the paths are very familiar. While I was looking at Gary's website, I saw the offering of a cruise where he would be teaching. I wished I could go, but knew I had just gotten out of debt and did not want to go into debt again to attend his studies. I explored the section of his website for where he would be appearing. I glanced down the list – Mexico, Costa Rica, Massachusetts, Arizona, Texas, etc. All of these places were not very easy for me to attend. As I got to the next to the last place he was appearing, guess what I saw. Yes, you got it! Gary was going to be at the Unity church whose website I had been looking at earlier.

Of course, it was months away before he would be appearing at the church near me. I wanted to read his first book *The Disappearance of the Universe* in order to gain more reassurance that my journey was not so strange and that there were others going through this same sort of experiences.

First, I opened up a new tab to search online for his book. For various reasons like not having my credit card available and not wanting to wait for it to arrive in the mail, I didn't purchase it. I decided that I would go to the local Books-A-Million store and get a copy. When I got to the store, I went to the dreaded "New Age" section. I was sure it was NOT going to be in the Religious section. Even though the experience that Gary was writing about, like mine, was very religious. I mean what could be more religious than Gary's "out of time" visitors telling them about their experiences with Jesus!

Have any of you ever looked at the "New Age" section of a book store? This one in which I was trying to find

Gary's book was divided alphabetically by the author's last name. I was used to that in the fiction section of a library, but this section was sub-divided into sections like "Dream Interpretation" and "Wiccan"! So, here was a shelf almost half as long as the store subdivided into numerous categories where each section was mostly arranged alphabetically by the author's last name with the occasional book reshelved in the wrong place by some uncaring customer. It was a nightmare to try and find Gary's book there! I kept looking, because I was embarrassed to ask for help in the "New Age" section! While I was looking, Depok Chokra's book *Jesus: A Story of Enlightenment* caught my eye. It was one of those books that was not shelved in the correct place, because I saw 3 or 4 of the same books below that. I opened it up and read what the book said it was about. I have always been curious about what happened to Jesus during his early years. You know the ones after childhood and before he started doing the miracles the Bible tells us about. So, I took it with me as I walked up front gathering the courage to ask about Gary's book.

When I got up there, I asked if they had a copy of Gary Renard's book *The Disappearance of the Universe*. The sales person said he did not and asked if I wanted to order a copy. I replied that I did. He put in the required information and told me it would be there the following week. I was disappointed that I had to wait that long, but I was there and ordered it along with purchasing Depok's book. Even at that stage of my spiritual journey I was beginning to realize that God wanted me to purchase that book.

I read Depok's book and found his ideas at the end about how to manifest a closer relationship with God. Depok's ideas rang true for me. By that I mean, here is a man raised in a different religion than I was and writing about what I believe to be universal truth. There is one God and many paths to become closer with Him, but all of those paths lead to Him. I mean, why is it that so many people look at the differences? Why don't we look at the similarities? Why don't we see that each of us is one of God's precious Children? Okay, Tana, get back to the story.

I was impatient about not being able to read about Gary's journey while studying *A Course in Miracles*, but I waited until the day after I was supposed to have received the automated call to come to the store and pick up the book before inquiring about it. Since I was in town the day after the book was to have arrived in the store, I went by and inquired about it at the sales counter. The sales person looked it up on the computer. She said that it would not be in until next week. Now, at times like this in the past I would have been furious that a store who makes its money from selling books could not get a book within 2 weeks, especially when I could have ordered it online and received it within days! But today, I giggled inside with the thought that God is very funny! His plan and mine were not the same. But, I was trying to listen to Him in order to experience more of His Love, so now when things seem to me to be going wrong I laugh inside. Now I am laughing with His Joy, because I know He is in control of my life! He will not lead me astray. My path is directed by Him. It is much easier and a much more peaceful, joyful journey to experience than the road I used to take which was very stressful and angry.

I continued to wait each week for the phone call to come to tell me to pick up the book. I didn't bother to go by and check anymore when I went to town. I now knew God needed me to complete a certain portion of this book He had told me to write without any influence from Gary's book of this same type of journey. God had let me read enough of Gary's book on the Internet to assure me that this journey was not to be fearful, but not any more of it than that until I had finished about 50 pages of mine. I am gradually beginning to not pay any attention to the ego's voice telling me that God is a vengeful God. I am now listening to God tell me through all of the wonderful things that have been happening to me and my family and friends that He is the God of Love! I have nothing to be frightened about when I am in His Hands!

Well, you guessed it! I was finally able this fifth week of the journey to sit down and read about someone else's spiritual journey while reading *A Course In Miracles* and training the mind using its Lessons. Boy, I am glad to read about someone else's journey! And, yes I am very glad Gary is braver than I am by being able to receive visitors in bodily form from God. Though, sometimes I wish I could ask Arten and Pursah some questions I have. I'm still working on the releasing of all fear thing, so I'll just continue to be happy with that small quiet Voice that I hear for now!

9
Week Six

God, how do I experience on earth a little more understanding of what Your Love is?

Self: God, thank You for all of the experiences you have had me go through on this journey, but especially the most recent ones!

Self: Okay, I'll play this "human game" and pretend You don't already know what I'm talking about. I know you are All-knowing, but I'll go through them for You.

Self: You're welcome. The first one I want to thank You for is the seeing with my eyes closed at night. You know I've thought I was seeing everything in my bedroom at night even when I shut my eyes. At first, I couldn't believe it was happening! So I would put my fingers on my eyelids which in my ego's fear would not allow me to still see. I mean at night you see in mostly shadows anyway, which made me think I was not really seeing with my eyes closed. But last night when I went to bed after reading part of Gary Renard's book *The Disappearance of the Universe*, I closed my eyes and saw the details of my room in the dark very clearly. And then, I realized what You've been trying to tell me on this journey in different ways. I do NOT see with my body's eyes! I am only seeing the projection that my mind on a different higher level has me see!

Self: Yes God, I am glad I finally got that message, too. And when I did, I wasn't afraid of seeing something that in the past would have and did frighten me. In fact when I realized what You had been saying, I laid there and giggled inside with the realization!

Self: Oh yes, there was that other sign you gave me along those same lines. Of course, I did not really like the way that sign began!

Self: Well You know, I had to experience that awful headache when I woke up. I went to the bathroom and asked if I should take some pain medication and heard You say, "It will not hurt." I took it and went back and lay down. I did my Rules for Correction. I forgave myself for dreaming I had done something to think I deserved this headache and thinking I was separated from You, yet my head kept pounding. I felt like I still had to read some of the text of *A Course in Miracles* and did my lesson. I even did the work I had to do in the online class I am presently teaching. All the time my head kept throbbing, even after an hour was up and the medication should have taken care of it. I lay in the bed and cried. I asked You what I should do. You said to go take a bath. Now God, I know it was You, because I wanted to take the bath later after I had gotten sweaty and completed the housework I had planned to do that day. But, I am learning to listen to you, even if I don't always remember to ask You what I should do and go ahead and plan my day like I used to do without knowing You are always in my life and available with a much better plan than mine!

Self: Yes, You know I listened to You and went and took the bath. I lit my candle like I always do and began to fill up the tub with water. I turned off the overhead bathroom light and got in the tub before it was full and turned on the heated jets in order to put my head in the warm water hoping it would help the pain to lessen or go away.

Self: You know what happened. I looked around and saw everything in that bathroom as if the overhead light was on! Last week when I got in the tub to wash my hair it was so dark from the light of the one candle that I couldn't tell which bottle was the shampoo and which one was the conditioner! In fact, just the other day when I lay in the tub to talk to you for the required 10 minutes from my lesson from *A Course in Miracles*, I couldn't even see the hands on the clock to know if I had been quiet and listened for Your voice for that amount of time or not. But now, I could clearly see the clock hands and the words on the bottles! I giggled as I lay there, and my head was not pounding any more. You know I thought. "Yes, I get the message loud and clear! I see with the mind's eye and not the body's!"

Self: You're right again as always; I received another message with that sign! I had asked You what to do and then followed your directions even though it did not coincide with what my plan was. But did I have to have that awful headache?

Self: I guess You're right. Sometimes we have to experience painful lessons to learn. I mean this whole "separation illusion from You" thing is painful! I can't wait until I learn all of its lessons, so I can come Home to You!

Self: Right, You want me to tell You what else I learned. Well, I learned that since I asked You what I should do and did what You asked me to do, then the bathroom being lit with light is a sign that I am beginning to see more of the spiritual light I am supposed to be seeing with instead of what I think my body's eyes see. How did I do?

Self: Okay, I will encapsulate what I think I've learned. Here goes. If I want to experience a little more of what Your Love is like (even though experiencing what Your Love is really like is only possible in Heaven with You), then every moment I am to practice forgiving everyone who does anything that seems to take away my peace. I am to do nothing but forgive them for appearing to do something that bothers me along with forgiving myself for thinking I am separated from You and feeling guilty about thinking I could ever really have left You and my home. I should bless them and let You make the correction on a higher level.

Self: I'm glad I've got that part right! And today I've learned, very painfully I might add, that I should ask You what I should do. I should not plan for the day. I know you don't mind if I go to the bathroom or get something to eat. You just want me to ask for Your guidance, because Your plan is the only one for returning Home as soon as possible.

Self: Okay, until next time we talk. Boy, I hope I learn these lessons quickly, so I don't have to experience those painful headaches again anytime soon!

Self: Wait? You mean we're not through for today.

Self: Gotcha, we are through for today, but not with this lesson.

Self: You need for a little more time to pass, so I can truly learn this lesson, and we'll talk about it tomorrow morning.

Self: Got it. I'll talk to you then.

Next morning, same lesson

Self: You're so funny God!

Self: You're welcome. I know you expect this journey to be joyful, because you keep me giggling!

Self: You know why I'm laughing. Your lesson from *A Course in Miracles* was about sickness like my headache!

I just wished I hadn't needed the time interval to learn this lesson!

Self: Okay, you want to know what I learned from it. Like Lesson 136 says, **"Sickness is a defence against the truth."**

Self: Yes, I know what the truth is. The truth is I am not a body. I have never left my home with you and my brothers and sisters. We are still at home with you as One. All of this is an illusion perpetrated by the ego with my will to do so to make me think I can ever be separated from You and Your PERFECT LOVE.

Self: You're right as always, of course. The ego is getting frightened that it is going to disappear, because I'm becoming more "right-minded" or practicing Your love here by forgiving others and myself for thinking we are separated from You, learning to listen to Your Voice, and being guided by You in making all my decisions. So the ego sent me that headache to say, "See you ARE a body. You have a pounding headache! Is that real enough for you? Where is your Loving God now?" I only had the headache when I listened to its voice, but once I listened to Yours, it subsided. I know I have a long way to go before I get all of this right, but I appreciate Your gentle and constant encouragement to be more like You.

Self: Oh yes, if I get sick again I'm to say just like Lesson 136 says to do.

> "I have forgotten what I really am,
> For I mistook my body for myself.
> Sickness is a defence against the truth,

But I am not a body. And my mind
Cannot attack. So I can not be sick."

Self: I am so glad You sent me that next lesson! You could not have had better timing (like You could ever have anything but that)! I'm ready for the next lesson tomorrow. Until then, love You!

Events of Week Six

This week started off slow as far as God bringing forth miracles for me to tell you about. It seems like this part of the journey is more about me trying to describe the inner, personal journey which is much more difficult to do than describing the miracles that someone could see with the bodies' eyes. But before I got around to telling you about that, I got a call from my friend Autumn.

Like many other of my friends I have described to you earlier, Autumn was my colleague before she became my friend. The last year in which I taught in public school in my role as Instructional Lead Teacher, I spent most of each school day with her in her classroom trying to help her figure out how best to successfully implement the new more stringent math standards that Georgia had delegated its students to master.

Since I had spent so much time with her and we had become so close, I did not understand why God did not want me to send her a copy of the beginnings of this book. I was so worried about her getting her feelings hurt when she found out the rest of my friends at school had been in on it from the first. I would try to force God to give me a sign by mentioning Autumn's name to our mutual friends in conversation, but I never got the second sign that God usually sends me to send a copy of what I had written to her. It was probably another one of those hard things that I felt like God had asked me to do in this journey, yet I waited for the sign to confide in her what I was doing.

Finally last night I heard from her! She called because she was so sad with missing our friend Jeanie who had moved a year and a half ago to a different state. Autumn had been helping her son Jason with his Facebook page and had seen Jeanie was on Facebook at the time. They "IM"ed each other for a few minutes, and this had left Autumn tearful. I was so glad Autumn called, but also shared her sorrow in missing the day-to-day contact with Jeanie. We talked for about an hour on various subjects, but mostly the alternative school and our mutual colleagues and friends.

After we had worn the subject of school completely out, I asked her how her son was doing. That was another thing we shared. Both of us had only one adult son and had pretty much raised them on our own. Both sons had suffered with depression and at different times had abused alcohol and other drugs. Yet, the older our sons had gotten, the fewer difficulties they both faced with these issues (Thank God, that they do grow up and learn their lessons!).

So, I was surprised when Autumn told me that Jason was facing one of those crises in life which makes your life very unsettling and unhappy for a time. As Autumn began to cry again and describe her worry for him, I knew God was ready for me to reveal to Autumn about this book. We spent the next half hour talking about the book and Autumn's experiences about asking God for signs and then listening for God's response.

I knew that Autumn's faith in God was very strong! I knew that some of what she would read in here would go very much against what she believed, but knew that God would guide her as He always had. When we were talking about the signs to know if God was talking to us, she related to me a couple of her personal experiences.

Autumn told me that she got married as a young teenager. When she started thinking about divorcing him, she was very concerned because she didn't believe in divorce. She consulted her minister, who said she needed to ask God for the answer and tell Him what kind of specific sign she wanted to have Him manifest. So, she asked God to tell her if she should get a divorce or not. She told Him to send her the money for the divorce, if that is what He wanted her to do. A couple of weeks went by, and she received a check in the mail for $3000. It was from an unexpected source and was more than enough for the divorce. Autumn knew that was her sign and obtained her divorce.

There also was a time when she didn't have enough money to feed her son and stepdaughter. Autumn said she didn't have enough money for a box of grits (now in the South, when you say that it means you don't have a penny on you). She prayed again to God to help her feed her children. The next day she got a check for $50. These stories show you that Autumn knows the power of talking to God, hearing His voice, and receiving His Love and Blessings!

Here I was worried about her getting her feelings hurt, and God was waiting to use me to deliver a sign to Autumn that God has a better plan than ours and for her to know that everything is going to be all right. We spent most of the latter part of these conversations laughing and remembering God's joy instead of the ego's temptations to make us believe that our miserable and painful experiences are proof that deny our power to live this part of our journey joyfully as Children of God!

By now, you know that many times there is something else that is "strange" that happens in my stories (Thank God!), and this one is no different! A couple of days after my conversation above with Autumn, Jeanie calls. Remember Jeanie is spending all her energy in raising her great-granddaughter, so she doesn't have much time anymore for us to talk on the phone. Since we had had a very long talk earlier that week for the first time in a long while, it was unusual for her to call me. She said her great-granddaughter was occupied for a moment and she just had to tell me about her "strange" experience with Autumn.

When we had talked earlier in the week, she told me she had sent Autumn 2 or 3 emails and had not heard from her. I had not talked to her since she visited me here, but told Jeanie that our mutual friends had said she was fine.

Jeanie said in conversation today that the night in which she and Autumn had "IM"ed on Facebook had happened very "strangely". She had lain down with her great-granddaughter as she does each night. If she doesn't lay down with her and rub her back, then she won't go to sleep for a long time and Jeanie wants her to be well rested before she has to get up the next morning and go to school.

While she was lying down with her great-granddaughter, "something" made her get up and check her email. She usually does not do anything during this time as not to wake her great-granddaughter up, but she got up and went to her computer. While she was checking her email is when she and Autumn had the brief "IM" conversation.

Jeanie kept repeating that "strange" was not the right word for the experience. I giggled inside with joy, because I knew she was listening to God and doing what He wanted her to do. I know **God has promised his children wonderful things, and He will bless us with His abundant blessings!**

Part 3

Communion

10
Weeks Seven and Eight

God, how do we learn to listen to Your Voice as a spiritual union?

Self: Mornin' God! Here I am ready to do Your bidding, so what's next?

Self: Oh, no! I hate to go back to the way I was when we first started this part of our journey together, because I know I have learned your plan is better than mine. But God, this is another one of those things that is going to be difficult for me to do. I don't want to be the one to second guess you, but are You sure this is what I need to do next?

Self: Yes God, it was only a couple of days ago! You were right, as always, when you had me wait to tell Autumn about the book. She needed it later, not at the beginning of the journey.

Self: You're right again God; Autumn was with us at the beginning of this journey together! Her mind was with the rest of ours from the very beginning, and with Jesus in the lead we are bound to be going down the right path!

Self: I am your obedient child, and you have NEVER led me astray, so give me the details of what I'm to do next.

Self: Yes, You've only had me writing on this a couple of days a week and sending out what I've written in an email to the people You've told me to send it to.

Self: So if I'm hearing you right, now You want me to email them every morning. God, are You positive that won't make them hit the delete button more before even reading it?

Self: I got it! They still have the choice of whether they are ready to hear Your voice or not with the delete button! Are we going to go through this process each morning of me trying to type what I think You are saying? You know, sometimes Your voice is so still and quiet that I'm not really sure I'm hearing what You really want me to say. It does angst me some! Not that I mind suffering a little. It's not anything like what Jesus and his disciples had to deal with!

Self: Whew, You just want me to copy and paste what I'm reading from *A Course in Miracles* that day.

Self: That's much easier! You, Helen, and Bill have already done the REALLY hard stuff. I mean ya'll worked on that for 7 years! I certainly am glad you told me to stop this book after 12 weeks!

Self: I hadn't thought about that, either! This means You want me to concentrate on only one lesson from the text from *A Course in Miracles* just like I am the Lessons! That will mean less time on reading, so I'm not really spending any more time than usual doing Your work! I really appreciate that!

Self: I thought about something else God. In the Introduction to the text of *A Course In Miracles* You said," It is crucial to say first that this is a required course. Only the time you take it is voluntary. Free will does not mean that you establish the curriculum. It means only that you can elect what to take when. It is just because you are not ready to do what you should elect to do that time exists at all. (You will see miracles through your hands through me. You should begin each day with the prayer "Help me to perform whatever miracles you want of me today.")." So, when I picked the book up years ago and read that, I took it to mean that each person gets to decide if they are ready for it or not. Aren't You taking away each person's free will when I send them a message each day?

Self: That's right, there is that old "Delete" button to deal with that! And, my ego's voice is so quiet now that I wouldn't care one bit if anyone told me to take her name off of the mailing list for the ACIM stuff. I can say for sure that at this point of my journey with You, that I am joyful and peaceful most all of the time! I'm so glad I listened to Your Voice and am going hand-in-hand with my brother Jesus towards You!

Self: God, You are so funny some of the times along with all of this serious stuff we talk about and do! I mean, I heard you very clearly say that I'm to begin a new section this week, but I really didn't hear what You wanted me to call this section. Then, this morning I heard the word "Communion". You saw me type it in. I know what communion means when I am in church, but was unsure about it for the title for this section. So, I right clicked and chose "Synonyms". My body's eyes went down and saw the synonym "spiritual union" for communion. When I saw this, I knew it was the one You wanted me to use, because I truly feel now like You, Jesus, and The Holy Spirit are on this journey with me and all of the others to which You have had me send out regular emails to!

Self: Right, what did I think was the funny part? You know! It was when I went to copy and paste the Introduction to *A Course In Miracles*. I was reading down further under the intro, because I've learned that I get a different meaning from what I'm reading depending on what stage of the journey I'm at. So, I'm reading and what do I see? You've got it! Down the page is the word "Communion"! And not only did You use that word, but you also used it to refer to Your scribes Helen and Bill's second phase of their journey with You, too. Here's what you said, "As soon as you (Helen and Bill) have entered the second phase, you will be not only willing to enter into communion, but will also understand peace and joy."

Self: You're right; I hadn't thought about that! Lately when someone calls me, another person, in this group of people I email everyday now with Your message, will call. Like the other day, I was talking to Waylon when Jaye called. I tried to disconnect Waylon and talk to Jaye, but I haven't figured out how to do that on the BlackBerry yet! So, I redialed Jaye. And then, I was talking to Jaye and Danette called! I mean I talk to Waylon almost every day, but Jaye and Danette call usually only once every couple of weeks! That doesn't seem like a coincidence to me! And then, earlier this week when my sister came down here to visit Dad and me, she called twice and both times I was about to pick up the phone and call her! And not only are these coincidences happening more frequently, but now we are laughing about it more. I do feel like as a group we are more connected and more joyful and at peace! Thank you, Father for the peaceful, joyful stage of communion into which we are entering!

Self: Father, I have a quick thing I want to talk to you about before I go do the "human" thing.

Self: Well a couple of weeks ago I was going in Home Depot, and I noticed that when dad and I went in the exit, that the alarm went off. Now I didn't think much about it that first time, because there was someone going out the exit at the same time with a sack as we were going in. So, I just thought that the cashier had not cleared the sensor that sets off the alarm on something in that person's bag that was exiting the building. That same day dad and I didn't find what we were looking for and as we were walking out the exit do You know what happened?

Self: Yes, You're right as always! The alarm went off. I thought about it for quite a while and wondered what was going on. So, yesterday when my sister and dad went back to Home Depot, I let them off at the door since it was so cold. After I parked the car, I went through the entrance and began to smile at the greeter. The minute I stepped over the threshold, the alarm went off. The greeter looked at me and could see I had nothing in my hands and only carrying a small purse. I just kept smiling and pretending that nothing unusual had just happened and walked on in. The guy behind me said I must have something in my purse that had set it off.

Self: You want to know what I had in my purse that day. I guess You didn't bother to see that on that day, huh. I have what I always have. I had my billfold with a little money, my credit cards, driver's license, and health insurance card. I also had my glasses in their plastic case in there along with the pen Danette gave me when I earned my doctorate degree.

Self: Oh, and Tylenol in case I get one of my headaches. You know me by now. I don't like carrying a big pocket book! When I think about it, I don't think any of those items would set off the alarm. The only other thing I had on me was my Blackberry, and if it sets off the alarm there would be many people who would also be setting off the alarm.

Self: Oh yeah, I went and found dad and Lynn and told them about it. We laughed. I said that maybe it had something to do with these vibrations God had sent me.

I mean, all of us are getting used to these strange things that happen to me.

Self: You know what happened when I left, too. Yes, I set off the alarm when I left. The sales girl looked at me trying to figure out what had set the alarm off. I could see she was puzzled, because I didn't have anything in my hands. I was alone again, as I was going to get the car to bring it to the section where you load your car with the items you had bought and had left dad and Lynn paying for the things we had purchased. I was also the only one leaving the exit door again, so I know it was me that set it off. Lynn wanted me to give her my phone and let her walk back through the doors to see if that was the cause when I told her and dad about it. It was cold, so we didn't try that theory out. I mean Father if you had to send me a gift, does it have to be one that makes everybody look at me as if I were a thief! Well, at least it is in just one store! I guess You can't tell me about why You've done that, can you?

Self: I figured not yet. I know there are certain things You can't tell me, as it would scare the ego too much. Oh well, I guess I just have to stop shopping at Home Depot. Man, that's a bummer! I love getting new things to finish the house! Oh well, that's a small sacrifice to make for spreading Your message. Is there anything else you need me to do right now?

Self: Okay, love You and talk to You later!

Events of Weeks Seven and Eight

This week I realize God is telling me we are starting a new stage of our journey together. As always, I hear the message in that small, quiet voice and do not really know what it means until something happens in my life to spark some recognition of His meaning. I know that my talking to Jeanie and Autumn at the end of last week has something to do with this new phase we are entering. Here are the signs that make me cognizant of it.

Remember how at the first stage of this journey I got directions to do things from God and fought with the idea of doing them? Well last week after conversations with Jeanie and Autumn I heard to paste a message from my reading of *A Course in Miracles*, because it would provide them with reaffirmation that what we had been discussing was a message through me from You. I had no problem that day with sharing God's message with each of them for a specific incidence, as it made sense to my logical brain. But, this week I've heard Him say to paste my reading from the text of *A Course in Miracles* each day in an email to the group of people to which I am sharing this book per His instructions. Now, this is the first time He has asked me to do something that affects everyone, since He asked me to send out this book I am writing and to my logical brain this does not make sense.

Unfortunately, I am still not quite at the place at which I can just listen to what God wants me to do and put aside my judgments of what others are going to think about what I am doing. I so wish I was there! You see somewhere in my mind I KNOW I would be better off, yet my ego's voice is still not completely gone. So, it does still bother me when God asks me to send to my family and friends what I am reading from *A Course in Miracles.*

I ask myself why that is. I know *A Course in Miracles* was scribed by Helen and Bill as told to them by Jesus. I have no doubt about that, especially as I am having that same sort of experience. I do not hear inner dictation like Helen did, yet somehow I do not have that much trouble sitting here and writing this in what others would consider a short amount of time.

I think it bothers me to push my beliefs on other people. I have always felt like my beliefs are my own. Maybe that is because I believe in organized religion and churches, yet what I heard in those institutions did not always "jive" with what I believed was God's message. I mean the God I loved would have to love me more than my earthly parents love me and more than I love Waylon. Now, that has to be a whole bunch and with a much greater love than I can imagine! And, the things I heard in church when I used to go, like you are going to "burn in hell" and some of you will not go to Heaven, did NOT sound like a loving God to me. At that time in my life it was either stop going to church or do not believe in an all Loving God. I chose to stop going to church and to not tell people who went to church (like everyone I know almost) what my beliefs are.

A few years ago Waylon told me that I might like Joel O'Steen's message, so I watched him on TV. The first time

I heard Joel speak, I immediately thought, "Yes! That is the message that the loving God I believe in would want one of His messengers to deliver!" I tuned in many times to listen to Joel speak God's word. He always backs his message with the Bible and speaks of God wanting His children to have His blessings. Joel gave me faith that in today's world the God of Love is speaking! Since then, I have attended churches with female ministers who speak more of God's Love. You see, I've told you that I am a positive person which makes me want to hear more about God's message of His love is with me all of the time! I do NOT believe that you have to instill fear (opposite of love) to motivate anyone to do what is right and Christlike!

Okay, I got off on a tangent. Sorry about that! Anyway you have a little more understanding about why I did not want to paste a message a day in an email to my family and friends. Of course, I did what God told me to do, and this was the first sign that we are entering a different stage of this journey.

The second sign came the other night. That night I had done my nightly meditation reflecting on the lesson from *A Course in Miracles* and listening for God's Voice and had checked my phone to make sure I had been doing it for the required 5 minutes. Yes, it was 10:40, and I had meditated for at least 5 minutes. I set my phone to only alert me if someone called, because I did NOT want to have one of those emails that told me my paperless bill was ready to be viewed to wake me up in the middle of the night. Usually, I am so at peace after the meditation that I drift right off to sleep, but not that night. I lay there and tossed and turned for over an hour and a half. I thought about what I had eaten or drank that might have had caffeine in it, yet could not think of anything that would keep me awake. I asked Jesus what I was supposed to be doing that I was not, so I could do it and go to sleep.

Finally, I reached over and turned on my bedside lamp and picked up my Bible. I read random pages for a half an hour or so. Most of the pages I chose did affirm that what I was doing by choosing to be a messenger for God was right. I know the pages I read were really not random, but I also knew the message I was supposed to be getting was not to be found in there.

After exhausting that avenue for God's message, I heard the message to check my email on my phone. I thought for just a nanosecond that I had checked it right as I went to sleep and could not imagine why I would need to check it again. By now, I know to do what that small, still voice tells me to do. At 1 AM, I was ready to do anything to get some rest! I leaned over and picked up my phone and found an email that had been sent at 10:45 with a subject heading of "I'm torn".

The email was from Ann, who is like a daughter to me. During these difficult economic times, her job had been cut. She was asking for my advice about what she should do. I replied immediately to her email. I started off with telling Ann that the only advice I could give her was from where I was on this journey of trying to hear God's voice tell me what I should do. I reminded her that when I think I hear God's voice, I usually ask for a second sign from Him to confirm that the first sign was from Him. Of course, I gave her the Tana spiel, also. My friends know what that is. I tell her how wonderful she is (which she is- as all my friends and family are- aren't we all His children and created in His image) and reminded her of her particular talents. I also told her it would be okay, because God had her back and would guide her in the right direction. He would make sure she had everything she needed and not to worry. Once I sent the email off, I was able to drift off to sleep. The next day, I had a brighter email from her where she told me that she had had "way more than 2 signs" to point her in the right direction!

Another thing that has happened this week is that I have begun discussing what I think my beliefs are with family members. You know the ones. The ones that are different from the typical beliefs about man's interpretation about what God said in the Bible. For example, Waylon wants to know if the separated individuals we think are saying things in our life's script know we are making up things for them to say. I told him that I'm not really sure yet how all of this works. I do believe that we have thought we could be separated from God and are acting out these human lives like we are. I do believe we have never really left our home with God and that all of us will return home to be with Him once we all realize that fact.

I've also spent a couple of days this week reading what I have sent out in emails to my sister. Remember that she has ADD. She has a difficult time understanding what she reads, so I read some of the text from *A Course in Miracles* aloud and we discussed what we thought it meant. I realize this is in preparation for when I have to talk about what I have learned, and it is helping Lynn gain more meaning from His words.

A few days later my vibrations changed again. I'm sure if I had a device to measure them, I think they would be at a higher frequency. I have come to realize that how I fulfill this role He has given me changes a little when that happens.

Since Ann has emailed me about what to do about the direction she needed to take when her job was cut, I should have realized that the vibrations meant that more phone calls would follow that were along that same vein. And, those phone calls did come. Not only did they come, but when I would be talking to one person another one would call at the same time. That seems to be happening more and more frequently. I believe it is because at some level all of the individuals with which I am on this journey are communicating with the Holy Spirit and Christ as One. For me who wants to talk to whomever needs me, it sometimes makes it difficult for me to decide whether I stay on the line with the first person who called or do I try (because I still don't always connect to the 2nd person on the line on my Blackberry) and talk to the other person on the line.

Okay back to the part about my next phone call. It was from Danette. She wanted to talk about – guess what? You, got it. She had been reading signs that were requiring her to change jobs the year after next which would be the year before her oldest daughter would enter middle school. Again I had to say to her, as I had said to Ann, that if God was sending more than one sign to receive God's blessings, she would have to do as He was directing her.

While I was on the phone with Danette, Waylon called. So, as soon as I got off the phone with Danette, I phoned him. All of you know he has been struggling with money from what I have already told you earlier, and things have not changed. He has received money from his jobs, but by the time they have stalled him for so long his profit has been eaten up. Waylon told me he didn't understand. He was praying regularly for the people for whom he worked to pay him on time, so he could provide for his family and pay the people to which he owed money. From where I am on this journey, I said to him that maybe he was getting his answer. I was interpreting God's message to be that Waylon was not supposed to be in construction. I asked him what he would be doing if he could do anything he wanted to do. He replied, "Mom, you know I've always wanted to buy and sell cars! I would love to buy an upper end car, drive it a while until it sells, and then buy another one to drive. In fact, I would love to do the same with grading equipment!" I reminded him that God wants his children to experience nothing but peace and joy, so he needed to look for the signs to figure out what that was!

For 2 nights after that, I couldn't sleep. I would ask God to tell me what He wanted me to do, yet could not quite figure it out. I would pick up the Bible again and open it to read verses. One of those verses was from First Corinthians verses 4-14 which basically says that those who do God's work have the right to make a living from it.

I texted Waylon with the verses to give him another sign from God. The only other verses I read were confirmations for me to realize I was doing what He wanted me to do. On the morning after the 2 nights of little sleep, I read my lesson and then read the next lesson in the text of *A Course in Miracles*. When I got through reading the text, I thought about how difficult it must be for some of the group to read that much and understand it. The school teacher in me wanted the people in my group who learned best auditorally to hear that message.

"How could I send God's message to them, then," I asked myself. Last year when my computer died while I was teaching an online class, I had ordered a new one. I knew it had a built in camera and had used it once after I had gotten it, but not since then. I opened up the video camera program and began reading the text from *A Course in Miracles* into it. That was no problem. The speed reading lessons my dad had provided me, really helped out with that part. So, I typed my usual message to the group and added I was sending it in a video form for those who preferred that method and began to attach the video file. For those of you who are tech geeks, you probably realized it was too large. I thought if I tried it again and blacked out the entire background including my face (which would make me much happier- as I really didn't want people seeing my face), then the file would be smaller and maybe I could send it. So, I spent the next few minutes repeating what I had done earlier with the screen completely black. To my deepest regrets, that didn't work either.

I did not give up, because I felt like this was a step God wanted me to take. If He had put me in charge of delivering His message to my family that shared my blood and those connected to me in Christ, then I knew it was important to have it delivered in a different medium other than the written word. I kept searching on the computer for a program that would allow me to do just the audio. Finally I found one! I still don't understand why a search for "audio" didn't bring it up. I mean, who would search under "sound recorder"? Anyway, I read the text for the third time into the software program and was able to upload and send it to everyone.

In a couple more days, The Holy Spirit directed me to ask for reflection about this journey. I am so far into this journey that I didn't think twice about asking for it. A few weeks ago I would have been anxious about what people would think about me asking for it, anxious about what it meant if I didn't get a reply, and anxious about what they would reply. But not today, I just sent out the email. I realize now that I am on my journey and that everyone is going to eventually get there with me. It just might not be at this particular time. In other words, my journey now most of the time is filled with peace and joy as God intended it to be!

While I was waiting for any feedback, Carol, the special lady in my brother's life, called. During our conversation she told me how much she enjoyed hearing my voice read the text from *A Course in Miracles*. She said it made it much easier for her and Jaye to understand it. YEAH! She also said she wished I could have read her bedtime stories as a child. Thank you God, for sending Carol to tell me that I had heard Your message!

Waylon, who never liked homework assignments, was the first text I received with his reflection. He wrote, "I have been searching and worshipping false idols (money) since I can't remember when. I'm on a search for happiness now which has nothing to do with money!"

As his mother, who has always told him that his happiness has always been the only thing I wanted him to achieve, reading that message increased the joy in my heart by tenfold!

All of the things that have occurred during these 2 weeks have made me reflect upon what all of this means. I have now come to the conclusion, that this part of the journey is leading me to take a more active role in relaying God's message to my family and friends and not just expecting them to absorb what I had learned by just reading this book that I am writing. I know that this group of people along with me is being prepared to do something together. God is using me to do that. I am okay with that. I am now more than just okay with it, in fact. If all of the people on this journey with me can receive God's blessings like I have, then let's go!

11
Weeks Nine and Ten

God, how do we learn to give and receive Your Peace that passes all understanding?

Self: Hello, Father. What do I need to do today?

Self: Okay, I can do that! I **am** learning to trust and obey what I hear You say, but would you mind repeating exactly what it is You want me to start this message with?

Self: So, You want me to say that You have one important message that **must be learned**. That message is to receive Your peace we must always see each and every one of Your children as Jesus Christ saw them. Exactly how does my brother, Jesus, see us?

Self: Oh, Jesus sees us just as You created us in Your image. He knows that each of us is one of Your children and not a one of us has left our Home with You. When Jesus looks at anyone, he knows that we are perfectly sinless. But, God, how can we be sinless? I mean even though I have travelled on this journey for a while now and have tried to treat everyone like my brother like you have told me to, I still get a little upset every once and a while when I do not see my brothers and sisters as You created them.

Self: You're right God. You always remember, but the part of me that thinks I'm in this body still forgets. You're reminding me that what I am seeing in this body when I perceive a brother as a body is **not** the way You created him. I am seeing through this "projected body that I created's" eyes (when I thought I could be separated from You) a brother who created a body with the thought he could be separated from You. But, the truth is that none of us could really be separated from You. Thank goodness, you sent The Holy Spirit with us to keep reminding us that this is not who we really are!

Self: Oh yeah, since these bodies are not really in the image of You, then we have not really done bad things and sinned. Like You said, we can think of it as would we accuse ourselves of doing bad things just because we dreamed we were doing something horrible. Why God, that's insane!

Self: You're right, that's what You just said. Accusing ourselves of sinning is an insane idea, because this experience in bodies is not who we really are, it is only just a bad dream.

Self: So God, how do we get out of this bad dream and experience only Your Peace?

Self: Oh, that's what You have been trying to tell me. Okay, I'll be quiet now and let You talk.

Self: Let me see if I've got this like You want me to write it. Jesus saw each of us without the body. He saw only the perfect image You created. He always blessed each and every one of His brothers and sisters. He never attacked anyone and any record of such was just a misreporting of it, because You say that Jesus and his message was always one about Peace, Joy, and Love. Is that it?

Self: You also want me to stress that it is important to receive peace that we must give peace and the only way to do that is to never judge people. We are always to just bless the person with our thoughts or send out signals of love and let you give the other person an attitude adjustment at Your level. Anything else?

Self: That's really easier for me to not get upset and let You handle it! It will save me much energy! If only I could remember that every time I want to tell someone off that messes my peace up! It's still difficult, but God I promise to keep on working on it. I have the motivation of knowing that each time I let you handle it on a different level that I'm getting closer to You and our home! Who wouldn't keep working harder for that kind of reward!

Self: Before You go, I want to thank You for showing me Your message everywhere I look.

Self: Where? You know television, music, movies, books, websites, and almost anywhere I look now I see or hear Your message.

Self: Specifics, okay I can do that. I've already been specific about music, but let me say at this point that any song that has the word "love" in it I see as Your love now and not romantic love.

Self: Movies, well I LOVED the messages I know you were giving me when I watched *Avatar*. I mean when I first read its synopsis, I thought of Your biblical hero David when he fought Goliath. But, when I saw the end where all of the Na'vi were joined together along with their power Source and making miracles happened that made me think of how You keep telling me that I have to realize that we are all One with You in creating like You. I had huge tears of happiness when they made Jake real in his Avatar body. I thought that You were telling me that one day I will come home and have the love and freedom to do miraculous things like the Na'vi did.

Self: I forgot to thank you for the song *I See You* from the movie! I did a lyrics search for it and found it on http://lyricsmusicvideo.blogspot.com/2009/12/leona-lewis-i-see-you-lyrics-video.html. I think all of the words are meaningful and beautiful but these words from it touched my heart the most:

And my heart was never open
And my spirit never free
To the world that you have shown me
But my eyes could not envision
All the colours of love and of life evermore,
Evermore

Self: Yes You're right as You always are, I haven't talked about TV yet. I hear many of your messages in the stories on TV that are like the ones I have been getting from You. When I watch *Heroes* I see more light streaming across the screen. I don't think the cameramen that shoot these episodes are blinding people's faces with streams of light! I don't remember that much light on the screen before I began this journey with You. I mean I can see a message that we are like You and more powerful than we realize. I know we are in these bodies and that You know all Your children can be heroes and deliver your message to everyone that comes into their lives and save one another by joining together for a certain purpose. I get that, but I don't quite get the so much light thing. Unless, you are just always giving me signs to remind me that all of Your children are more like You and the Light of the World than we are aware of.

Self: Yes, there is another TV program that I see more light than usual in. That is *Caprica*. I can see the themes in that one, too. There is the theme about One God which is against what the majority of people believe on the planet Caprica. I can see the parallels to most people not realizing that we are One with you even here on earth. It also has the theme of having an avatar which can do things in a virtual world that can't be done in the real world. I know this one has some strong messages in it from You, because I have seen the characters' noses just stream off into a beam of light. It was very cool! Anyway, I just wanted to tell You how much I appreciate You reminding me of Your love all of the time by sending me the signs everywhere I look! I hope it means that I'm getting closer to You by trying to use Your love all of the time in every situation and do what my brother Jesus would have done! Thanks again and until the next time I talk to You, bye.

Events of Weeks Nine and Ten

You remember how last week I told you I knew that this journey was changing, well this two weeks has brought way more signs than I can chronicle in this book! One of the first ones started with my trying to watch a movie I had recorded on the DVR. It was Sunday afternoon. I am teaching two online classes to have a little extra money to travel with my Aunt Jean in May, so I needed mindless TV to relax. I had just chosen a bunch of movies from Saturday's listings and programmed them into the DVR to be recorded. That way I knew I would have some choices. I was in such a state of wanting something totally mindless that I selected the sappy love story from the Encore Love channel. I found it on the list and pushed select. A black screen appeared on the TV. I hit the Play button thinking it was paused, but nothing happened. Sometimes when this happens, I've found if I try the whole process again it will work. So,

I went back to the list of recorded movies and pushed the Select button for the second time. Again there was a black screen, and again I pushed the Play button to try and get the movie to start playing. For the second time, I was disappointed. As I am going on this journey to hear God's voice, I have begun to recognize more quickly that He was talking to me. Lately when technology doesn't work for me, I have begun to take that as a sign there is something else I am supposed to be doing. That day I listened to what I thought God was saying to me, and I went back to the list of movies. Near the top was one titled *The Ultimate Gift*. I knew that one was the movie God wanted me to watch, so I pushed play and of course it worked right off the bat!

Basically the movie was about a spoiled, rich man whose billionaire grandfather had died. If the young man wanted to receive his grandfather's gifts, then he had a series of tasks to perform to be worthy of the ultimate gift. I can see now that in this story that God was telling me that he was pleased with me. I had listened to His voice and was trying to do what He wanted me to do. He was sending me a sign that His blessings had begun to be felt in my life, but they were nothing compared to the Ultimate Gift he had in store for me and anyone else that chooses to listen to Him and follow His commandments!

I decided to watch another movie. I told you I really needed that stress relief that day! It was also one of those rainy, cold early spring days which were made for just that type of activity. I looked at the titles. I decided not to try the sappy love story, either. The next title that caught my eye was *Safe Harbor*. This movie was based on a true story about a couple who thought they were going to retire and travel around the world in a sail boat as soon as they got finishing restoring it. Instead a juvenile judge kept dropping off young men at their sailboat. He would ask them to keep them for just a few days, because he said the juvenile detention center was overcrowded. Now you know what happened in those Hallmark Channel movies, they ended up keeping the boys until they were prepared to go out into the adult world and be successful! In fact, they took in more boys and named it *Safe Harbor*.

I felt like God was telling me that I know I thought I was going to retire and travel, but He had a different mission for me. I feel as if He is going to lead me and my family in Christ to create a place for young people who need a temporary home until they can go out into the adult world and be successful. You see, the school teachers going on this journey with me and I have seen many such young people as students in the alternative school where we work. It seems like in this world we live in today, that there are many children whose parents or parent are unable to provide them with the emotional and physical environment in which children best thrive. They are not bad people or bad children, but in need of help. These parents love their children, yet they just can't provide them with what they need at the time.

I know that is what we're supposed to do, because – you guessed it – I received many more signs than just the movie. In fact the next day Waylon called. I was telling him about how I couldn't make the movie play from the DVR and then told him about the movies I had watched. He said, "Mom, that is like the *Hillsong* group. They have homes for children in many places all over the world!"

I received another sign when I talked to Jeanie later that week. She asked me if I knew anything about the Schools in Malls. She had heard about them the night before from her local news channel in Knoxville. Now, she didn't know anything about what had happened to me over the weekend and the movies I had watched, and there she was telling me about schools that are different and trying to make a difference with at-risk kids! Do you think I've had enough signs about this? I don't know what this journey's going to bring, but I am excited about what blessings God has in store for me to receive and to give!

Speaking of listening to God and knowing it is Him when technology doesn't work for me, I was listening to a podcast by a couple who writes and talks about the inspirational books they have published. I was trying to listen and do some research about them at the same time. When I would put their names in Google and hit the search button, I got a message that it couldn't find it at the time. So, I just thought God was telling me that He was sending an important message in the podcast and that I should pay close attention, as He knew I was not good at listening and doing something else at the same time. As the podcast got to be nearing the hour mark, I tried to look them up again on Google. Again, I received that message, and again I just listened to the podcast. After the podcast was over, I went to search about the couple one more time. This time I realized the Internet was down completely at my house! How had I listened to that podcast during that time? I guess it was downloaded already! I really don't know enough about how all that works, yet I am sure that God will make sure I get His message! I even was at peace about not having the Internet working, even though I knew I had to have Internet working to teach those two online classes the next day! The next morning it still wasn't working, but I got on the phone and went through all of the steps to try and get it working again. It was to no avail, though. The entire system in my area had been down for hours. The service rep had told me that someone would call from the local station to work on my problem. Again, I was still at peace with what was going on. Ten weeks ago before I was on this stage in my journey with God, I would have been freaking out with not having the Internet and having two classes for which I had responsibility for teaching! Now, I just think that God's plan for me is better for me than mine and hold on to the peace that He sends me! I did receive service before lunchtime, so I didn't have to go to Starbucks and drink expensive, good coffee while using their service to teach my classes! **I thank God for making sure I am receiving His peace that passes all understanding, since I am trying so hard to be the child that listens to Him and does what He is asking me to do!**

12
Weeks Eleven and Twelve

God, what else do You think is important for us to hear from You at this point in the journey?

Self: God, first of all today I want to thank You for directing me to write this book. I mean, even though it scared me at first, I now am joyful to get up and write the words You inspire me to put down here.

Self: I can't believe we are almost finished with this book either!

Self: What do You mean when you say we're not finished?

Self: Oh, we're finished with this book, but You've just started getting out Your message for Your people here in the 21ˢᵗ century. But God, You've already written that fabulous book, *The Bible*, isn't that what You want people to read and live by?

Self: I see what You mean. People have misinterpreted some of Your messages in it and then used it to back up some actions which are not the loving ones like You would have us do. Okay, I can see that, so what do we do to know Your Word?

Self: Is it that simple? Each of us just needs to spend quiet time each morning and evening being quiet and listening for the message You want us to receive. Is that all we need to do?

Self: Your children should also read books like the one I am writing now, too? But Father, they are reading this book now! I certainly don't want them looking to me for all of the answers!

Self: You're right as always, Father. You are talking to everyone all of the time, if they just take the time and listen. And, I can tell that more and more of Your children are writing books about their intimate experiences with You, because You keep directing them to find their way into my life to read. But God, how do we know it is inspired by You and contains the message You want us to hear?

Self: Again that seems to be too easy! Each of us will know if it rings true to us as Your Words. Yeah, I've found that out in the books You've had me read. All of them have the themes of sharing Your Love with all of Your children, and all of them stress that we are all one with You. But, one of the books stresses the need to take care of our bodies and another one says our bodies are not of consequence, so which do I do?

Self: Oh, I should just follow the one I think rings most true to me for the path I'm on in which You are directing me. Is there another way to hear Your words?

Self: That sounds like fun! I would love to be in God's Book Club! Each of us could read a different book inspired by You and then discuss the one we read with our friends. Then we could swap them and/or get more and do it all over again. I can't wait to get started with that part of the journey with You! Okay, I've gotten off topic. What do You want me to do next?

Self: Of course, not only am I to read more books by other people who are inspired by you, but I'm to use the Internet as a tool to communicate Your message. I am so glad You are finally using mass communication! I always wondered why you didn't use it like it asked in the musical *Jesus Christ Superstar*.

Self: You're saying that I'm to use the acronym for God Is Talking to Us as a title for the webpage. But Father, I don't know how to set all this up!

Self: You're right again. There I go worrying about the future. I know You will send me everything I need to get it done! I am practicing more frequently to be in the here and now and experience Your peace and joy, yet it seems like a lesson that I'm going to have to continue to work on. What else do You want me to write in this book?

Self: Yes, there is so much You want to say, but there comes a time when the readers gets too overloaded with so much material and then can't process it. Whew, for a moment You had me scared! I was beginning to think this book was going to be too heavy to carry around even in paperback form!

Self: I also like Your point about people needing to read different people's chronicles of Your message, as that will show more of Your children that You are talking to everyone! You've already inspired Danette to write a book for teens, and she's gotten off to a good start. I loved the part where the teenage girls need to decide if they are more like Cinderella, Snow White, or Sleeping Beauty! I guess that means I'm finished with the book writing for You though, right?

Self: I should've known that answer was coming! You will inspire me to write another one, but I need to have some balance in my life which means I need to take some time off and then come back and start another one.

Self: I was really kidding! I love doing what You ask me to do! You've rewarded me so for being Your good and faithful servant! I will gladly follow You to the ends of the earth! Oh wait, I was going to do that anyway! Goodbye, love You, and until the next time we talk!

Events of Weeks Eleven and Twelve

"I am so excited that the last 2 weeks of which I am supposed to write about in the book are finally here," I thought when Week 11 finally began. I was positive something miraculous was going to happen to finish off the book and wow the readers! The vibrations coursing through my body had increased their frequency again. Wasn't that another sign? The buildup had been there, too. It had begun when Danette had called on one of her drives home from school. That was the best time for us to talk.

We chatted for a while like we always do. During the conversation the book came up as it has since this part of our journey had begun. I told her I was at peace with what would happen to finish the book, but that I was having difficulty waiting until that time to arrive for God to reveal what I was supposed to write.

I reminded Danette that God had had me clear my schedule from teaching any online classes for the next two months and knowing me I would want and need something to do during those months. I was going to take a trip with Aunt Jean during the second month. I told her that my sister Lynn suggested that I take that Mexican cruise with Gary Renard and be a part of the study groups he was going to have during that week. After reading his book *The Disappearance of the Universe*, I had wanted to have an opportunity to be face-to-face with someone who had been through an experience like

I was having while following the prescribed lessons from *A Course in Miracles*.

Danette knew I did not like traveling alone. She also knew that the only person who would enjoy and want to take that trip with me would be Jeanie who couldn't come with me even though she had been invited to do so. After she heard me tell of Lynn's suggestion she said, "I don't think you are supposed to go on the cruise. I know what you should do. You should come up here and we should get together at Debbie's house. That is our spring break, so maybe we can all get together."

Hearing her say that thrilled me through and through. It had been more than ten months since I had seen my friends from school and more than two years since I had seen Jeanie. These were the people God had directed me to include in this journey from the beginning, and what Danette had suggested seemed a plausible suggestion to me. I replied, "Yes, that sounds right to me. I mean the last section of the book is titled *Communion*, so I'm sure that has to be what we are supposed to do."

She immediately responded with, "What? You've got to be kidding me! I hate to tell you, Tana, but I haven't had a chance to read any of the book for the last couple of weeks and didn't even know that!"

When she said that, I knew this was a sign from God that her suggestion was the one from Him that we were to follow. I asked her to make the arrangements for this, since she saw the majority of those people during the work week. I also reminded her that I was not supposed to be the one that leads the group all of the time. I was okay to start it, yet I knew that a well-working collaborative group must share in all the responsibilities. I had mentored Danette for years to lead the group at school, and now it was her turn to do so with this group. She agreed, arrived at her home, we said our good-byes, and we hung up our phones. I was so relieved to let someone else take that responsibility for just a little while and thought about how hard it had been for Jesus who always had to shoulder all of that responsibility of leading all of the time!

Now that time had arrived to go to the suburbs of Atlanta and be with them, I could hardly stand the waiting any longer. It had taken some arranging for me to get to Atlanta, though. The weekend before the meeting time, Carol had invited dad and me to come to Jaye's house to spend Easter, so we were at Lake Seminole in dad's car. My car was in Atlanta with Waylon who had borrowed it while his truck was being repaired. Dad and I were to meet Lynn in Cordele and have lunch. Afterwards, dad would continue on to the coast and I would go with Lynn to stay at her house for the week and pick up my car.

When we had made the plans, it had seemed to be so easy. I'm so learning that when I make plans that things can seem to go awry even if I think they are what God wants me to do and therefore should go well. The first problem was that dad was not feeling well at all. The new house's location brought different pollens, so dad and I both were fighting their allergies. He had contracted a virus the week before the pollen began raining down upon us. He assured my sister and me that he could complete the journey home once we finished our lunch. So, we let him and proceeded to continue our trip to Atlanta.

When we got a few miles from Atlanta, the traffic backed up on I-75. Have any of you ever tried to come from south of Atlanta on that route? It was awful! Lynn looked down at the temperature gauge of the car and said it was running hot, so we got over into the right lane and inched forward until we could get off at the next ramp and see about it. The good thing was we both knew all of the back routes from where we were.

Now at this point you have to know a little more about the car. It was my mother's '91 Lexus. It had over 270,000 miles on it, but it was a Lexus. Lynn had just gotten it back a couple of days before. It had needed a new transmission. She told me she felt as if mother was still with her in that car, and she never wanted to drive another one. At this point, I was trying to convince her that mother would not want her driving around in a car that was unreliable. The temperature gauge had gone down a little, but was going back up into the hot range again. We decided to pull off the road and let it cool down. After it did, we tried to make it closer to Lynn's house. We went a little further, yet again the gauge jumped back up to hot. This time we could pull into a gas station. Lynn went inside to buy some coolant, but they were out of it. There was an AutoZone store across the street, so she walked over to try to get some there. She came back, and we put the coolant in it per the instructions.

Lynn had called her husband at work, and I had called Waylon who was working on the computer on a plan to submit for a job he was doing. Waylon said he wanted to come help, and I wanted him to let us try and get it resolved before he drove through the traffic for miles and leave his work. So after putting in the coolant, we got on the road again. We watched the gauge carefully go back and forth. We found if we could avoid traffic and keep the car moving that it did not stay in the hot range as much. Finally we made it to her house and went inside to cool off, as it had been in the mid eighties that day.

The strange part about all of that experience is that I was pretty peaceful through it. If that had happened four months prior, I would have been panicking all over the place. Yet, I am learning that God has a reason for everything that happens to us. I try to stay in the moment and not worry about the future, because I KNOW God's plan is better than mine. Because I was at peace, my sister was more at peace even though she was worried about maybe having to make mom's car a new piece of yard art.

The good news we got later from the auto repair man was that the car did not need to become yard art! It was the water pump that needed replacing. Because the water pump is in a place where the timing chain must be taken off, Lynn and her husband decided to replace it, too. They knew it had needed to be replaced, yet had not wanted to spend the money. Since they were going to have to pay for the labor of it with the water pump, they decided to spend the money for the timing chain. Lynn and I feel it was God making sure she could depend on the car. Now she had a new transmission, water pump, and timing chain in mom's car. We were positive she could drive the car for another 100,000 miles.

The time prior to the meeting with my friends from school was spent happily hanging out with Lynn. We had so much fun shopping, eating out, going to the movies, and just being together. The day I was to meet my friends at the Mexican restaurant near Debbie's house for lunch, I loaned Lynn my car to go to the pain doctor's office to see the PA and get her pain medication for the month. Lynn reassured me she would be back in time for me to go. I was not worried, but I knew she was. I spent the time getting ready to go. She came back home about 30 minutes before I needed to leave apologizing for being later than she wanted to be. I told her it was no big deal. Then she told me about what happened to her in the doctor's office.

Lynn said that she had watched the people who had come into the doctors' office after she had arrived go back into the cubicles before she did. She knew those people had appointments before hers, but had not gotten to the office on time. She had tried to not let it bother her, yet she knew she had my car and I had plans. When she went up to the window, there was a woman in front of her who wanted her 2 o'clock injection for pain as soon as possible. The nurse asked her if she had taken her pain medication. The woman replied that she did not have the money to pay for the prescriptions. My sister told me that something told her to ask the lady how much the prescriptions would cost her, so she did. The woman replied that if she had $10, then she could get her prescriptions. My sister got out a ten dollar bill and handed it to her. Immediately the lady hugged her, thanked her, and blessed her. She asked for her address, so she could send her a thank you letter. Lynn gave her the address, and the lady left wiping tears of joy from her eyes. And, Lynn said that the nurses were crying, too. In fact one of them came out and hugged her.

Lynn and I talked about how her blessing had been given back to her. At the doctor's office, she had been given one of the first appointments for her next visit. She would not have to wait the next time. She also knew that everyone in that office would do everything and anything to help her, as she had helped the woman in pain.

The other blessing she had was the one of the feeling it gave her. The day before we had heard a guest on the *Dr. Oz* TV show tell people who fight depression to do one kind deed a day for someone else. Lynn has taken antidepressants for years. It is evident to me that she is now working on other ways to make herself experience some of that joy that she knows God has promised her is hers for the asking. **When anyone loves God's children as He loves them, then God's love is given back to her tenfold!**

After our conversation at eleven, I left to go to the restaurant. On the way I got a message from Jeanie on my phone. In it she detailed why she couldn't be there. There was way more than just a couple of signs from God to say she needed to stay at home. I was sad, as all of us were, that she couldn't be there, yet elated that she was looking for signs!

When we all got to the restaurant, we heard that Autumn couldn't come either. Her life was filled with other kindnesses she had to do for others instead of spending the time with her friends. Again, I was disappointed and again I knew Autumn was right where God wanted her to be.

The time we had together was filled with laughter. I can't remember when I have laughed so much in a long time. When it was time to leave, I was a little disappointed that I did not feel that there was anything that had happened that was going to put a big finish to this book. I hadn't seen anyone's body form a stream of light into Heaven like Gary Renard had seen when he looked at his wife one day or anything like that. Danette had asked our friends to share how going on this journey had changed her lives, and it was evident that everyone was beginning to try and hear what God was telling her to do. Yet, when I left I was still puzzled about how God was going to have me finish this book.

I followed Danette home to spend more time with her and to see her soon to be two year old son Max. I missed seeing her other two children who were with their grandparents at their great-grandmother's house in Tennessee, but was delighted to have time alone with the two of them.

I was also delighted to be able to take my son and his family out to eat for his fortieth birthday. You see since my son has become a man, I have missed most of his birthdays. It almost always fell on my spring break which meant I went south to see my parents during those weeks.

The last day I was in Atlanta, I got up and went early for Waylon's wife Dana to trim my hair. When I left there, I called Waylon back. I had heard his Calypso ring tone while I was in the chair having my hair cut. He was at my lake house measuring for boards to repair the dock. I told him I would meet him at Home Depot to purchase the materials for it.

While I was waiting for him, I decided to browse the books in Books-a-Million. I looked at the fictional section but did not find anything that really caught my eyes. I strolled through the Christianity section, yet again nothing really jumped out at me. Finally I found the New Age section hidden in the back. It always makes me a little sad as I arrive in that part of the store and become cognizant of the fact that I think God is talking to people today in the 21st century and the books he inspires are relegated to that place! There are rows of shelves with different versions of the Bibles that contain His words from a couple of thousands of years ago which do contain a wealth of information that is still relevant and important for some people to read, but they were written for a people whose lives were very different from us and needed God to direct them more. They did not have easy access to books and a number of them could not read, so some of His meaning is lost today after all those translations.

I just don't understand why it doesn't ring true to everyone that if what God said in the Bible is true, then why wouldn't everybody believe that God is alive today and inspiring more and more people to write about their experiences with Him. I mean today you can write a book in a Word document much easier than ever, and then you can send it anywhere in the world instantaneously through the Internet. Why wouldn't God the Creator of All use mass communication if He wanted everyone to hear His message? Why wouldn't He use it for everyone to realize they can hear Him, because other everyday people like me can tell about her experiences with Him through it?

Sorry, I went off on a tangent again! You know by now how I can do that. Okay, I'm looking at the couple of set of shelves with the New Age material and not the fortune-telling or witches stuff. My eyes scan over the book titles and authors. I've read some of them. Some are useful for the journey on which I'm going and some are not. My eyes finally rest on a paperback called *Tomorrow's God – Our Greatest Spiritual Challenge* by Neale Donald Walsch. It has a plain white cover and black letters, but it calls to me to pick it up. I scan it and find some of the messages that ring true to me that I have found in *A Course in Miracles,* Depok Chakra's and Gary Renard's book. I also see one of Walsch's books entitled *Communion with God.* Since this section is similarly titled, I looked at it, too. It did not sing to me in the same way the first book I picked up did, so I decided God wanted me to take the first one I chose home. I took it up to the counter and purchased it.

I took my new book to the car and as I sat in it waiting for Waylon, I began to read. The messages I got in it were ones I so needed. I would read a little and tears of joy would flow down my cheeks, because I knew God was talking to me through Walsch's words. I also knew that God had sent me the inspiration to finish this book. This is the miracle I needed to tell you about. If you are listening to God, loving everyone as His children, and doing as He directs you to do (the things that are easiest to do and bring you peace and joy); then He will bless you with what you need to bring you peace and joy just as He did for me when I read *Tomorrow's God*.

I've also learned that I can't plan what I expect God to do, as I did when I expected ostentatious miracles to happen at our meeting. I'm learning to find peace and joy in the now. God does not want me dwelling on the past. In His eyes, none of his children have sinned. All of us have made mistakes which we need to correct. We have not shown God's Love to others or ourselves all of the time, but we all will learn to do this and return home to God. It doesn't matter what color our skin is, what culture we align ourselves with, what gender we were born into, or with whom we share our sexual proclivities with; all of us are one with God and will go Home to be with Him!

I've learned that God also does not want us to worry about the future. If we truly believe in Him, then we have to have faith that He always has our best interests at the heart of all of His plans for us. If God has what is best for us happening each and every second, then we all should be smiling all of the time! I'm learning to do that too for myself! The more I make feeling God's Peace and Joy a habit in each second of each day, the more of His Joy fills my heart until now my heart wants to take wings and fly to sing His message to all who are ready to listen to it! Are you ready to hear His message? I hope so!

In fact I hope that you are able to answer affirmatively to all of these:

God, are you talking to <u>me</u>? - The question I know is an affirmative for all of God's children and that you know after reading this book is true for you.

Are <u>YOU</u> listening? – The question to answer affirmatively, so you can receive all His blessings and pass them on to all of God's Children!

Are <u>YOU</u> filling all of your moments with God's Peace and Joy? – The question to prove you have faith that His plans for your future are what is best for you, so you can receive His Peace and Joy!

Afterword

After completing the writing of this book, I continue to go on this spiritual journey of learning how to die into God. I am learning how to hear The Divine's Voice more clearly and accurately through my Spiritual Guides and Angels. I am sure I will write another book chronicling the events in my life, but I know that now is not the right time. I have completed two books for children that I know will be ready in the near future. For now, I wake up in the early mornings with a simple melody playing in my head and the beginning of words for the tune. The first song I completed is a perfect synopsis for this first stage of this spiritual journey on which I am traveling. I hope you enjoy it and may God Bless you each and every One!

Coincidences

I don't believe in coincidence anymore.
I just know that He's showing me a door
To a path that with a leap of faith
Leads me to His wonderful Pearls of Grace.

And each time that I see a hummingbird
Coming into my field of view
Well, I just take it as another sign
Of all the love in the entire Universe.

I don't believe in coincidence anymore.
I just know that He's showing me a door
To a path that with a leap of faith
Leads me to His wonderful Pearls of Grace.

And each time that I hear my cell phone ring
And a friend's voice is there to cheer me on
Well, I just take it as another sign
Of all the love in the entire Universe.

I don't believe in coincidence anymore.

I just know that He's showing me a door

To a path that with a leap of faith

Leads me to His wonderful Pearls of Grace.

And when a song comes on the radio

That has the message I needed at the time

Well, I just take it as another sign

Of all the love in the entire Universe.

Yes, I don't believe in coincidence anymore.

I just know that He's showing me a door

To a path that with a leap of faith

Leads me to His wonderful Pearls of Grace.

And each time that a book comes to my hands

With the words that I needed then to read

Well, I just take it as another sign

Of all the love in the entire Universe.

I don't believe in coincidence anymore.

I just know that He's showing me a door

To a path that with a leap of faith

Leads me to His wonderful Pearls of Grace.

Bibliography

"A Course In Miracles ~ Online Searchable Urtext Version," accessed September 23, 2010, http://coursein miracles.com/

Chokra, Deepak. *Jesus: A Story of Enlightenment*. HarperOne, 2008.

"Leona Lewis – I See You Lyrics N Video," Video and Lyrics, accessed September 23, 2010, http://lyricsmusic video.blogspot.com/2009/12/leona-lewis-i-see-you-lyrics-video.html

"The Master Teacher of A Course In Miracles," accessed September 23, 2010, http://www.themasterteacher.tv/

Renard, Gary. *The Disappearance of the Universe*. Hay House Inc., 2004.